DEATH IN MIND

Death In Mind

William X. Adams

www.psifibooks.com

KDP ISBN: 979-8-9877761-8-6

Contents

Table of Figures

Acknowledgments

I thank my teachers, dead and alive, for the intellectual foundations on which to build this structure.

I thank my friends, family, and colleagues for the social world that supports my journey.

I thank my lucky stars for living in a historical moment and circumstance that enabled me to think these thoughts.

I thank my Planck Code for a life tensioned between membership and alienation.

Preface

This essay attempts to naturalize death. You might think it's already natural. Everybody dies, always has, and nobody has ever not died. What could be more natural than death? But those are observations about other people, people who one day ceased moving and were pronounced dead.

From personal experience—mine, yours, anybody's—nobody really knows what death is like. You have to be alive to have experience, and if you're alive, you haven't died yet. In the context of personal experience, death about as "unnatural" an event as anything could be.

In fact, death is not an experience. It's the end of experience, the absence of experience. Nobody knows what it's like to die (near-death experiences don't count) because nobody has ever "come back" after dying, fanciful stories aside. Nor has anyone ever communicated with "the dead" to learn what it's like—again, putting aside mythology, religious doctrines, and paranormal tales. As a topic for first-person investigation, death would seem to be a dead-end.

That's certainly what I thought until I discovered numerous tiny Black Holes of Non-experience, later deemed "Black Holes of Nothingness" (BHNs) within the processes of normal mentality. I documented those in an essay called "Mind Without Brain" (Adams, 2021a) and provided detailed description of them in "Nothing in Mind" (Adams, 2023a).

Those micro-BHNs are unnoticed moments of non-experience, periods when one is not present to one's self. A larger, easily-noticed example of a BHN is dreamless sleep. Every night, you literally lose your mind for several hours. You repeatedly enter a period of non-experience, where your self, your "you-ness," your very mentality, simply evaporates. You become nobody, not located in time or space. Mentally, experientially, you cease to exist. It's normal. Normal, but very odd.

There are many other examples of BHNs in everyday life. They're everywhere, once you start looking for them. Anesthesia is one. A drunken blackout is an example. Tiny BHNs even occur in the middle of conversations and in the middle of thoughts.

On the assumption that BHNs are basically all the same, it occurred to me that maybe death is the biggest BHN of all. If that is correct, dreamless sleep, meditative emptiness, coma, anesthesia, and the micro-BHNs of ordinary experience are no different in principle than death. Except for the fact that we recover from all the other BHNs, whereas death seems to be a one-way trip.

Since death is terminal, it does not afford any obvious way to investigate it from a first-person point of view. To be clear, scientists from pathologists to paleontologists examine dead bodies from every which angle, but I'm not talking about bodies. I'm talking about experience: "what it is like" to have experience. There is nothing it is like to be dead, because in a BHN, the "you" is gone so there's nobody to experience anything. A BHN is the opposite of experience. It is "noxperience." (That's a term I've coined for whatever mental process the opposite of experience is).

If death is structurally and functionally the same as other BHNs, we should be able to learn something about it by examining those other, more accessible cases. BHNs of the everyday kind *can* be examined. Not by direct introspection, since there is no first-person point of view in a BHN, by definition. However, we can use scientific introspection (Adams, 2020) to inspect the context and horizons of BHNs. With several other methods, including functional analysis and a method called the MPM (Adams, 2023a), we can even get a glimpse of what's inside BHNs.

Needless to say, none of this is traditional science. Science is not designed to investigate mental experience. Science is organized around observation of objects and events in the world. Experience, made of mental phenomena derived from "what it is like" to encounter the world, is not susceptible to the scientific method.

Just for one extremely simple example of why this is so, we note that there are literally no "inner eyeballs," so self-observation of the mind is beyond the scope of science by definition. Introspection is not defined for science. A BHN logically cannot be an object of traditional scientific study.

I have described instead alternative first-person investigative methods parallel to science that can be used to examine experience empirically. They are Scientific Introspection (Adams, 2020) and the MPM (Adams, 2023a). Anyone incorrigibly committed to the existing scientific method as the *only* valid epistemology will find that this essay leaves them adrift.

For others though, here's the outline of this project. First, I briefly summarize key facts and principles of the mental architecture I use in my discussions of the mind. That architecture is called the QMP schema and was described in detail in Adams (2020a and 2020b), and summarized in Adams (2023a). Then I recount the main features of a BHN as articulated in Adams (2023a). That background will give us a common language and lay out some foundational assumptions.

Next, I draw a perimeter around death as a mental phenomenon: what it is; what we know and what we don't know. We'll have to distinguish between the "experience" of death, which is the *end* of experience, and bodily decomposition. Those are very different definitions of death. This essay is focused on death as non-experience, not the bodily remains that go into the ground.

Inevitably, it is necessary to consider eschatology, a big word for inquiry into the idea of life after death. Short answer:

it's an oxymoron, a confusion in reasoned thinking. But it's instructive to ask why such a myth persists in human culture. Maybe it's just irrational denial of death, but maybe it's also something to learn from. It raises a pointed question: are there logical, phenomenological, or other evidential reasons to question the characterization of death as absolute oblivion? I think there are.

Assuming death is no different in principle than all other known BHNs, it follows that death is not a permanent condition. The key question then is, "What persists across a BHN?" We garner answers from study of ordinary BHNs and see how those could apply to the BHN of death.

If the best conclusion is that death is transitory, as all other BHNs are, we are forced to ask, "What's on the other side?" We turn again to close study of the micro-BHNs within the cyclical QMP mental architecture to come up with answers. We apply them to the BHN of death and see what the result is. The outcome is surprising.

Finally, we sweep up the debris of smashed assumptions arising from re-defining death as a BHN. Topics include replacing the image of "The Great Wheel" with the Necker Cube as a new geometry for death. In the end, we have a richer sense of the interplay between life and death.

William X. Adams

September, 2023

BHNs in Mind

The main strategy of this essay is to suppose that death is a mental Black Hole of Nothingness (BHN) then apply what is known about ordinary BHNs to what we know and believe about death and see what happens. The strategy assumes all BHNs are more or less the same. Review of the known characteristics of a BHN is therefore an important preliminary.

Not all BHNs are equally well-understood. The BHN of anesthesia, for example, is difficult to study from a first-person perspective because it doesn't occur very often. In contrast, the BHN of advanced meditation is controllable and repeatable and has been described many times through many centuries (Van Gorden et al., 2019). The BHN of dreamless sleep is common and eminently accessible but difficult to study because the cognitive faculties needed for analysis are diminished in the periods just before and just after it (aka "sleepiness").

I base my characterization of BHNs mainly on the micro-BHNs that occur in each cycle of mental activity. Those are too fleeting to be noticed by casual self-observation but can be studied using scientific introspection (Adams, 2020) and the Marco Polo Method, or MPM (Adams, 2023a). A preliminary schematic of the fundamental cycle of mental activity will allow us to understand the role and qualities of the micro-BHN.

The QMP Model of Mind

The simplest possible mental event is called the Quantum Mental Process (QMP). It has been described in detail in Adams

(2021 a & b). It is the smallest complete mental act that can be discerned. The QMP is visualized in *Figure 1*.

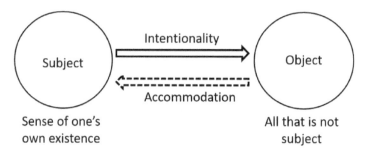

Figure 1. The Quantum Mental Process

In the first half of the QMP mental cycle, subjectivity emits an intentional act directed toward objectivity. The intentional act, a vector of mental motivation, generates an objectified representation of the just-prior state of subjectivity. That quasi-object allows subjectivity to (metaphorically) "get a look at itself," which is what makes introspection possible.

Objectivity itself is inert and unmotivated. Subjectivity soon "turns away" from the self-object, leaving it to become part of the not-self otherness of the objective domain.

In the second half of the QMP cycle, an object, or part of one, is accommodated back into subjectivity. Subjectivity (metaphorically) "recognizes" itself in the object, and reconfigures itself to include (partially or wholly) the object back into the subjective domain. That is a mental cycle. The cycle repeats as mentality continues.

That is an extremely brief summary of the QMP rotary engine. For details, see *Mind without Brain: A Proposal* (Adams, 2021a). The whole QMP cycle defines one mental event. A single thought is made up of many QMP cycles. While the QMP engine has numerous components, none of them, not even subjectivity, is itself is a mental event. Only a whole cycle defines a mental event. Mentality considered over time is a definition of consciousness.

BHNs in the QMP

One mental act is the base unit of experience but a BHN is a non-experience, so we do not see a representation of BHNs in the QMP diagram. But they are part of it and critical to the operation of the cycle.

At a whole-person level of description, a BHN is a period during which one is not present to oneself, a period of non-experience, no mentality, no sense of self or world, absence of consciousness: an experiential Black Hole of Nothingness. That's what you get, experientially, when the QMP engine of mentality stops spinning.

The QMP metal cycle ceases when subjectivity pauses its activity. When that happens, mentality disappears and a BHN prevails. Luckily for us, BHNs end and the QMP spontaneously re-starts.

When subjectivity emerges from the micro-BHN, it comes out "with its intentional guns blazing" so to speak, as if making up for down time, and the QMP is "on" again. That's why mental experience is actually bursty, not continuous.

Consciousness is not a "stream," as the famous metaphor would have it, but a punctuated, intermittent phenomenon more like Morse Code than flowing water. Several philosophers of mind have observed this about consciousness, though it is not the mainstream view. The mainstream likes streams. (Again, this is a savagely brief summary. See Adams, 2021a for details).

Why does subjectivity fall into a BHN between periods of intentional activity and why, after having fallen in, does it spontaneously emerge again? These are questions about the inner workings of a BHN. They were addressed in detail in a prior essay about BHNs, *Nothing in Mind* (Adams, 2023b).

A second micro-BHN occurs in the second half of the QMP cycle when subjectivity accommodates an object to itself. In order to accomplish accommodation, subjectivity inhibits its intentional activity for the same reason you have to stop talking in order to listen. When subjectivity exercises that self-control, it becomes inactive and falls into a BHN. When it spontaneously emerges, it finds itself reconstituted "on a larger footprint" than before. Its enlarged scope includes the former self-alien object within the expanded domain. At a whole-person level of description we say that we now "understand" the object; we "get it."

During the second micro-BHN the QMP engine is again paused, again punctuating experience with a moment of non-experience. The two micro-BHNs within every mental cycle are too brief to be noticed in casual reflection but are identifiable upon close examination. They can be mined for information about BHNs in general.

Modules of Mind

When we reflect upon our thought processes, we typically do not find the QMP model of mentality. Instead, we find images, ideas, words, songs, feelings, and distant memories. How does everyday experience map to the QMP unit of mentality?

Casual introspection reveals mainly only one aspect of the mind, the socio-linguistic part, which I call the SLM module. We take that to be "the mind," but it's only one third of the mind. A whole, mature human mind is composed of three modules, as shown in *Figure 2*:

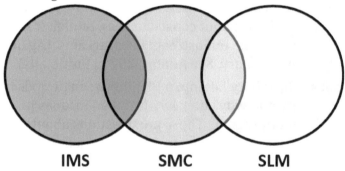

IMS   **SMC**   **SLM**

Figure 2. The Three QMP Modules of a Whole Mind

The three modules of mind are:

The IMS, the Intrinsic Motivational Source, supplier of mental motivation to the rest of the mind.

The SMC, the Sensorimotor Cycle, the feeling-basis for embodied experience.

The SLM, the Socio-linguistic Mind, the thinking and intersubjectively self-aware part of the mind.

Each of the three modules is an instance of the QMP architecture. The modules communicate and cooperate in the overlapping biscuits of the Venn diagram. The intellectual part of the mind, the SLM, is the only part of the mind capable of language and introspection. It has limited contact with its partner-in-mind, the SMC. It has no direct contact with the distant IMS module.

The Social-Intellectual Module (SLM)

The SLM typically believes it *is* "the mind," the entire mind, the whole of mentality and consciousness. Who will tell it different? The SMC, for its part, does not have language, cognition, or introspective capacity, so it is in no position to argue. The IMS has no direct contact with the SLM and cannot readily make itself known. The SLM's imperialism therefore goes unchallenged. That's why most people are not aware of their two other partners-in-mind.

The Sensorimotor Cycle (SMC)

The SMC module is the arena of body-centered mentality such as sensory exploration and discovery, attention and response, affordance and adaptation. The intellectual SLM conceptualizes such body-centered mental activities as feelings, desires, "instincts," pains, tendencies, and related embodied mental phenomena. Lightly conceptualized bodily phenomena can be further processed into explicit ideas, abilities, and skills.

A thoughtful person recognizes that the body has a "wisdom of its own" and acknowledges that conscious experience is a matter of cooperation between the thinking SLM and the bodily mentality of the SMC. This arrangement defines separate roles for intellectual consciousness and the tacit "lived experience" of embodiment.

The Intrinsic Motivational Source (IMS)

The IMS module is the least understood of the three modules of mind. It is the source of mental motivation for the whole system of mind. The intellectual SLM would disagree. It typically believes it is self-motivated. It chooses and decides, tries and relaxes, pays attention and ignores. But actually, it merely customizes the Motivational Force propagated from the IMS.

If you query a person (or yourself) relentlessly on any supposed autonomous motive, you find that at bottom, there is really no explanation for it other than vague terms like "desire." That's because what seems like self-determination to the intellectual mind is only the shaping of a more basic motivational force coming in undetected (via the SMC) to the SLM. The SLM customizes basic motivation to its own context, but the motivation itself is not self-determined by the intellectual mind. The source is a completely different module of mind, the IMS.

The three modules of the mature adult mind normally get along well together, so the intellectually dominant SLM hardly suspects it has two partners-in-mind. There can be hiccups and cross-purposes. The body often does unexpected things, like provide feelings and pains that the SLM doesn't expect, understand, want or need. The SMC often doesn't do what it's told, as any athlete will attest, causing frustration. Conflicting motivational expressions are the stuff of literature. But on a good day, the three modules of mind operate like a jazz trio.

The three-part model of the whole mind gives us language and concepts to make important discriminations generalizations about mental phenomena. This summary of the tripartite structure is severely truncated. Complete description is in *Mind Without Brain* (Adams, 2021a) and *Mind, Body, World* (Adams, 2021b).

How a BHN Works

In a previous investigation, *Nothing in Mind* (Adams, 2023a), the nothingness of a BHN was described as epistemological rather than ontological. That means the interior of a BHN is empty *not* because there's nothing in it, but because there's nobody to look at it. When you enter a BHN, you literally "lose your mind." The interior of a BHN is therefore empty because no point of view is available from which to experience it.

Noxperpience

Whatever does occur in a BHN is not experience. Instead, I have dubbed the invisible interior mechanics of a BHN "noxperience." Noxperience is something, not nothing. It is an essential part of mentality. But it is the opposite of experience, metaphorical "dark experience." It cannot be introspected.

Understanding noxperience faces a formidable epistemological barrier. To overcome it, I developed a special empirical method called the MPM (Adams, 2023a). Using that method, it was possible to determine that BHNs do perform essential mental work. In general terms, they are ontological transformers that convert self-relating subjectivity into brute objectivity, and back again. I imagine the BHN as a single process that operates both "forward" and "in reverse" to accomplish those transformations between mental subjectivity and objectivity.

We can affirm empirically that BHNs exist in the mental cycle and we can infer what they do, and state why they are necessary for mentality. Details are in Adams (2023a). With that basic understanding of everyday BHNs, we can apply the information to the "big" BHN, death. When we do that, some surprising results appear.

Death Vs. Other BHNs

If death is structurally and functionally similar to any other BHN, what can we learn about death that we didn't know? To make that comparison, we consider death as a first-person phenomenon rather than as a medical condition.

Scientific and medical definitions of death are about the brain and the body. Those are important, since mentality *is* embodied. But medicine is not capable of examining mental experience, so we must put aside medical ideas of death if we want to explore its psychology.

When we do that, we can see certain points of similarity between death as commonly understood in our culture and the structure and function of mental BHNs.

Similarities Between Death and other BHNs

1. Loss of Experience

As far as we know, death is the end of experience. All BHNs are mainly defined as periods of non-experience ("noxperience,"), retrospectively assessed. Building on that basic similarity, we can surmise with confidence that death entails loss of ordinary mentality and absence of consciousness.

2. Loss of Self

Death (as far as we know—I'll just assume that from now on), also involves loss of self. An important defining feature of ordinary BHNs is that one is not present to oneself, meaning that even the most minimal cognitive self-awareness is absent in a BHN. There is "nobody home" during a BHN, no sense of one's own existence, personality, memories, agency. Death too, then must entail the absence of self.

3. End of Time

In an ordinary BHN, there is no time. That is, subjective time is absent. After emerging from a BHN, one can deduce elapsed time from the clock, but there is no sense of time having passed while one was "in" the BHN. Personal history stops during a BHN. We presume the same holds true in death, which we say is "forever," though that's said by the survivors, who remain *in* time. More accurately, we should just say that death is timeless.

4. Loss of Embodiment

The main characteristic of death seen from the outside is the end of the body. That's pretty much what death means from both medical and common sense views: the body stops functioning and rots away. But what is the first-person, psychological correlate of that?

Psychological embodiment is more than just *having* a body. It is the experience of living *through* one. The central module of mind, the Sensorimotor Cycle (SMC) is the locus of one's tacit bodily mentality. It disappears when one enters a BHN, as does all the rest of the mind, leaving no basis for embodiment. We can assume the same is true for death. Thus, there would be no possibility of retaining any ghostly, "astral," spiritual, or other paranormal body after death because the mentality of embodiment itself is not present to support it.

5. Absence of the World

It almost goes without saying that the world and all its furniture and people are no longer present to a person in death. That's a solid assumption because the "first-person" is no more. The same is true in ordinary BHNs: No self, no world—not because the world ceases to exist, but because there is no one to experience it.

6. Abrupt Transition

The transition into an ordinary BHN is paradoxically both abrupt and gradual. You can "see" nothingness coming, as you fall asleep, so the descent is somewhat gradual. Yet it is not a continuous "fade to black." There is a sharp "lights out" moment when you are suddenly just gone. I have tried to examine the edge of that precipice to no avail. I can get close to the edge, maybe even dip a toe in and out the abyss, but the final plunge is sudden and the exact moment always unexpected.

More than once I have tried to pay attention during the onset of general anesthesia. I can feel it coming on. I imagine I see it like a herd of galloping horses drawing ever louder and closer. I watch carefully. But I've never seen what happens to those horses. I always disappear before they get to me.

We can guess that the onset of death is something like that. You expect it. You see it coming, closer and closer. But the Grim Reaper never gets close enough to show his face. You're "gone" before he gets there.

7. Loss of Agency

This is probably a consequence of loss of mentality in general. Falling into a BHN is ultimately involuntary. We "fall" asleep; we don't "jump" asleep. Loss of mental agency might be a consequence of cessation of IMS mentality that defines the moment of entry into an ordinary BHN's nothingness. It would be the same for death.

8. Anomalous for Survivors

We survive ordinary BHNs, and after coming "out" of one, we marvel at what just happened (or we should). There was a "hole" in the otherwise continuous fabric of experience. Every night, during dreamless sleep, you are not present to yourself for hours at a time. You cease to exist as a self-aware person. You evaporate from life and world. Seriously considered, that is a remarkable fact. Any BHN is a severe anomaly of life-experience, something far out of the ordinary, an unexplainable period of emptiness and nothingness. It's an astonishing event.

In the case of death, the survivors are other people. For them death is also anomalous, even though it is also very common. It's always a shock when someone dies. "I just talked to her yesterday!" we protest, as if that had any bearing. The idea that somebody we know intersubjectively could just evaporate from the face of the earth is anomalous, even though every single person knows it will happen to every single person.

9. Ignorance

We know something about ordinary BHNs, such as when they occur, what they are, and even a little about what they do. It's similar for death. We know it when we see it, and we have theories, of microbiology, evolution, and religion to explain it. But we don't really know what death is or what it's for. Likewise, we are profoundly ignorant about the functioning of all BHNs.

10. Evaluation

The micro-BHNs of the QMP mental cycle include an evaluative function. When an object is wholly or partially accommodated back into subjectivity, subjectivity's tacit goal of overcoming objectivity is "satisfied."

Accommodation is felt as "positive" feelings like satisfaction. Unsuccessful accommodation generates "negative" feelings like frustration. In the SLM module, more successful accommodation is "good." Failed or less successful accommodation is "bad experience." Details of the evaluative functions within the QMP are given in Adams (2020) and Adams (2021a).

Is there reason to believe anything comparable is present in the BHN of death? According to well-established cultural mythologies, yes. In the Christian tradition, for example, when one dies, one comes before St. Peter at the gates of heaven, and one's life is assessed to determine admission (Matthew 16:18–19). There is a similar judgment day in Islam.

In Hinduism, we have an evaluative function in the law of karma (*Rig Veda*, *Upanishads*). According to that law, one accumulates merits and demerits through one's actions and intentions. Upon death, the composite of those determine the quality of one's reincarnation.

Doctrines of being judged upon death are common throughout most religions, both modern and ancient, including those of ancient Egypt and ancient Greece. In Plato's Myth of Er *(The Republic, Book X)*, we see a panel of judges sitting before the portals to heaven and hell, judging each supplicant. The parallel between widespread cultural stories of judgment at death and the evaluative function of accommodation in ordinary BHNs calls out for further examination.

11. Rebirth

In many religions and cultural myths concerning death, we find the doctrine of reincarnation. After death, one supposedly is reborn to live again. This theme is less prominent in the Abrahamic religions, though in Christianity we have the example of the death and resurrection of Jesus, and the idea of "life after death" in heaven for everyone who passes muster. In other religions we see the idea that after death one re-emerges in a new body (a new "incarnation") to live another life.

In modern science, we say that one's body decomposes and is recycled into the elements from which all things are made.

That's not really in the spirit of reincarnation, which implies that something of the individual person's psychology persists across death, but the scientific story is not incompatible with that. The elements persist. We are stardust.

Do we find anything similar to the idea of "rebirth" in examination of ordinary BHNs? The plain fact is that we subjectively survive nearly all non-death BHNs (permanent coma might be an exception). Mundane though BHN recovery is, we should ask how it works, especially as entering a BHN entails complete loss of mentality.

Differences Between Death and other BHNs

The similarities between death and other BHNs are arresting and support the working assumption is that death is a variety of generic BHN. But there are some apparent differences that should be queried further.

1. One-way

The distinguishing feature of death is that it appears to be a one-way trip. We survive all other BHNs. In fact, if a person does not survive an ordinary BHN, we say they died. People "die in their sleep," and "die under anesthesia." They failed to come out of their BHNs.

We have some trouble distinguishing death from other BHNs in special cases of "vegetative coma." If suspended animation becomes a reality for space travel, we will find ourselves even more challenged to distinguish death and non-death BHNs. The main criterion now seems to be that if you survived the BHN, you didn't die. If you don't come out of it, you're dead. In-between, we're not sure.

2. Accessibility

Ordinary BHNs are susceptible to investigation. Even though they are periods of nothingness, the fact that they are repeatable make them open to study by various first-person methods. Death, however, only occurs once to each person, making it very difficult to study from a first-person, experiential point of view.

Even if one were somehow able to remain lucid during the Inward Fold of death, it would be impossible to report those observations because it's a one-way trip. We have numerous documented cases of "near-death" experience, but they are difficult to evaluate since the person did not actually die.

3. Fear

Most people fear death, which is not the case for other BHNs. Presumably fear of death is fear is of personal oblivion, separation from others, and loss of the world. Yet all that is common to any BHN. Even dreamless sleep, which everybody enters each night, involves personal oblivion, but few people fear sleep.

We strongly believe sleep will not be fatal. We have survived it unscathed hundreds of times, so we become indifferent to the fact that each sleep is an episode of non-existence. If you "died in your sleep" it would be just like any other night for you. The only difference would be that you wouldn't wake up, and you wouldn't even know that you didn't wake up.

Is habituation the only reason we don't fear ordinary BHNs? Some people fear general anesthesia because of the possibility that its oblivion could become permanent. Perhaps fear of death is really about the end of time. What we fear about death is its permanence. We're okay with *temporary* loss of everything: mind, self, body, others, and world. It's permanent loss we fear.

But what does "permanent" mean? When you're "in" a BHN state, there is no time, so for all practical purposes, it *is* permanent. There's no BHN clock ticking off the seconds until you "get out." Every BHN is "forever" from the point of view of the person who is in it (though that person does not actually have a point of view inside a BHN).

Apparently, we're not afraid to fall into oblivion as long as we expect it will only be temporary. We just don't want to be caught in there forever. Why not? What is it about the passage of time that we love so much? Time brings age, disability, loss, and death. But at least time postpones the inevitable: eternal nothingness, which we do not want.

It seems then, that fear of death is actually a love of time and change. That suggests that death differs from other BHNs in our attitude about time. Even though time is absent in all BHNs, death fails to promise resumption of it. We must examine more closely our beliefs about time to understand this difference.

4. Degree of Ignorance

Our ignorance about all BHNs makes death similar to the others. Even so, we know even less about death because there are no report-backs. No one who has ever died has ever communicated back to the living about what it is like. Woo-woo seances and fictional tales must be set aside. None has evidence that bears scrutiny.

During the late 1800s to the early 1900s, when the idea of "spiritualism" was popular in America, prominent psychologist-philosopher William James of Harvard made a pact with his brother, the writer Henry James, that whichever one of them died first, they would use all possible means to contact the survivor. Henry died first. William waited anxiously for weeks but heard nothing. Why? Did Henry lose interest?

Non-death BHNs are understood better than death. The meditative BHN, for example, is well-documented. It has been studied and written about for centuries by those who have experienced it. It is variously identified in the philosophical literature as Satori, Samadhi, Nirvana, and other names. Even so, that particular BHN is still extremely mysterious.

Other common BHNs, such as those of dreamless sleep, coma, and the micro-BHNs of each mental cycle are less-well-studied from a first-person point of view but are also strange phenomena about which we know little.

5. Alienation

Unlike ordinary BHNs, death is alien to us. We personify it as the Grim Reaper, and with ghost and demon imagery. That's not the same as fear. Even for those who don't fear death, it is still usually regarded as an "inhuman" or alien prospect, because death doesn't make sense in the context of life. It is the end of life, the negation of everything. We have no prior personal experience of death and nothing to compare it with, so it remains alien and other.

We do not regard ordinary BHNs the same way. Even infrequent and poorly understood BHNS like anesthesia or alcoholic "blackout" are treated with familiarity. The exotic meditative BHN is poorly understood in society, and might be regarded as a little weird, but is not considered as completely alien to humanity as the BHN of death is. This alienated attitude toward death inhibits first-person research into it.

Conclusion

In sum, death is strikingly similar to ordinary BHNs in multiple ways, but also differs from ordinary BHNs in a few important aspects. We need to explore these similarities and differences.

Death Defined

There are two ways to be dead according to the American Medical Association and the American Bar Association. One is to have irreversible cessation of all respiratory and circulatory functions. That is, the heart is stopped and the person is not breathing. The other is to have irreversible cessation of all functioning of the brain, or in other words, brain death. Those two standards have been adopted by all fifty states in the U.S.

The official definition makes death a biological concept, cessation of critical body functions. I have no objection to that definition of death, but this essay, like the others in this series, is about mentality, not biology. What is the definition of death from the point of view of mentality? Is dreamless sleep the same as death? Intuitively, we don't want to say that. But the official definition says nothing about it.

Physical and Mental Death

It seems likely that death entails termination of the individual point of view. That means it is not possible to be self-awarely dead. That conclusion is despite much folklore about chatty and scheming ghosts, seance-mediated communication with the dead, channeling of ancestors, and similar tales, all of which we can set aside for lack of scrutable evidence. In this essay, an important criterion of death is absence of individual mentality. That means no point of view, no subjectivity, no memories, no personality, no language or thought, no awareness or self-awareness.

Death has never been fully-described by first-person report. In the Bible, for example, Jesus returned from the dead after three days, but unfortunately, nobody asked him, "What was it like to be dead?" If somebody had asked, he might have said "I got really thirsty, but other than that, it wasn't too bad." Or maybe he would he have said, "I don't remember anything. It was like nothing."

In the absence of first-person reports, the surviving community defines what death is. That's the best we can do.

The Mind and the Brain

The prevailing community definition of death involves brain death. That's because of the very widespread belief that the brain causes the mind, or that they are the same thing. In this essay, as in the others of this series, I have avoided biological explanations for the mind. I seek an account of the mind based on first-person experience, not biology. If it is someday proved that the mind is indeed a biological product of the brain, these essays will become superfluous. Until then, we seek a mental, not biological explanation of death.

Most people, including most scientists, do not share that view. They tacitly or explicitly believe some version of the mind-brain identity theory. Common language in mass media uses the terms *mind* and *brain* interchangeably. "Brain" is a synonym for "mind." That's identity theory.

Identity Theory was articulated formally in 1959 by philosopher J.J.C. Smart. He asked a disarmingly simple question: "Is an experience of red a red experience?" And he answered "No." What did he mean?

Suppose a brain event happens that we label "the experience of redness." That does not mean the brain itself is red. Neurological activities don't have any color. Nor do brains. The brain is gray and white. Where is the redness of a red experience?

Smart said that "redness" is merely a label for the brain state correlated to that term. All mental phenomena are just words describing brain states, not separate things. Language makes it sound like "redness" is something different than biology, but "redness" is just a label for the biological condition. So-called experience is nothing more than words describing brain conditions. Thus, the brain, described by words, *is* the mind.

Smart does not worry about whether "there is something it is like" to experience red. He does not accept the validity of phenomenal experience like that. He only considers brain activity and the language to describe it. He also has no theory of how words acquire their meaning, what purpose language serves, why it is necessary to describe brain states at all, or who does the describing. His theory is very narrow in scope.

If Identity Theory were true however, we could confidently say that when the body dies, so does the mind, because really, there is no separate mind. Mind and body are the same. That is the default belief of our scientifically-guided community.

I find Identity Theory entirely implausible for many reasons I have detailed elsewhere (Adams, 2020, 2021a), but I'll cite just one brief argument here: such an explanation is self-refuting and therefore logically invalid.

To say that the mind is identical to brain conditions is a statement lacking a point of view. Brains, being made of fat, protein, and water, cannot have a point of view any more than a stone can. A point of view is subjective and mental, something a person can have but not a brain.

If a proponent of Identity Theory is a brain (and body) that has no point of view, there is no reason for it to express itself. Brains, like stones, have no intrinsic motivation or capacity to believe and assert anything. For that reason alone, Identity theory cannot be taken seriously. Asserting Identity Theory is like declaring "I do not exist." The statement is a performative error that undercuts itself.

Identity theorists are not susceptible to irony however and might retort that "a subjective point of view" is just the name of another brain state. That reminds me of Magritte's famous painting, *"Ceci n'est pas un pipe."*

Rejecting Identity Theory means we cannot say with certainty if biological death is identical to termination of the mind. We need a bio-independent definition of death to say what death means to a mind.

Mental Definitions of Death

When somebody dies, where does the mind go? We, the survivors, are the only ones who can say. From our point of view, death apparently involves cessation of the mind and all its intersubjectively-driven activities. Let's look at some of that process more closely.

1. Decomposition

Asking where the mind goes at death is misleading because "go" implies location in space. That's a metaphor. The mind cannot be fully located in space or time. From a first-person point of view, one's mind can travel to the depths and the outer edges of the universe and far into the past and the future. The mind is not bound by Einsteinian spacetime. Yet the mind can always be found where the body is, and that *is* bound by spacetime. So it's a paradox.

We sometimes say "I left my mind at work," but that's not intended literally—or is it? We are convinced that minds are embodied, connected to the meat that is our definition in time and space. The nature of that connection is unclear because sometimes we do mentally leave our bodies.

Decomposition of the body is a process by which it loses its structures and functions. Perhaps the mind ceases when it loses its structures in parallel with the decomposition of the body. That is a mental definition of death that respects the fact of embodiment without reducing the mind to biology. We can't say why physical death would lead to mental death but we can say the two realms of decomposition might occur simultaneously.

2. Presumed Dead

Another approach to mental death is to consider the person's residual persistence in community memory. We have "memorial services" for the deceased to allow the community to consolidate its collective memory. To the extent that we are all defined by our intersubjectivity, the survivors' memory of the dead person is an aspect of that person that persists beyond dissolution of their body.

Conversely, sometimes a missing person is "presumed dead." In that case, the minds of the survivors change qualitatively. They have decided the person is not coming back. The person's assets can be distributed. Their spouses can remarry, and so on. Being dead or not dead in the minds of the survivors has important interpersonal and social consequences.

An aspect of the mental definition of death then, is consensus among the survivors. They must agree that the person is dead or else the condition is indeterminate.

3. Loss of Intersubjective Connection

When the person is no longer "responsive," they might be presumed dead. This definition is about intersubjective responsiveness. The main form of intersubjective interaction for us is communication, especially with language but also with gestures, artifacts, touch, and other communicative acts. From "exchanging" communicative acts, we come to know what the other person means, intends, wants, believes, and so on.

It is not true that we infer the other person's mentality from their behavior. That is a common but erroneous belief I have debunked repeatedly in Adams (2020, 2021a, 2021b). Rather, we directly detect the subjective presence of the other person through the quality of their interpersonal activities.

Interpersonal communicative activity is the carrier of the intersubjective signal, much as a tune on the radio is carried by the electromagnetic wave. We don't logically or cognitively infer the tune from the wave. Rather, we appreciate the message directly and disregard its medium. In the same way, logical inference can be, but need not be part of intersubjective sensitivity.

Many years ago, I walked with a fellow graduate-student in a dimly-lit hallway of a university psychology laboratory. Back where the "rat-runners" had their spaces, we saw a bag of dead rats on the floor outside a lab waiting for pickup by an appropriate disposal service. There were about three dozen white lab rats jumbled haphazardly in a large, transparent, plastic bag tied at the top. They weren't bloody or mutilated. They had been "sacrificed" by the lab, as the euphemism went, probably suffocated with ether after their usefulness to science was done. Today, such crude disposal of the bodies would be highly unethical. There are strict rules about treatment of animal remains. Those were different times.

My colleague and I were from the other end of the lab complex. We worked on human subjects. We poked them and asked them questions, and showed them pictures, but we didn't put them in bags afterward. On this day we had wandered into the dark domain of a different culture. The bag of dead rats was not completely shocking for us, as we'd seen it before, but it certainly made us stop and look. My fellow student turned to me and asked, "How are these rats different than they were this morning?"

All I could say at the time was "They're much less jumpy now." We both knew that was not a good enough answer. I thought about that question for decades. Today, I would say that the difference was that I could detect only a very slight intersubjective relationship between the rats and myself. They seemed more like objects and much less like subjectivities than they would have before their demise. That's how they differed from their earlier condition. They differed intersubjectively.

The dead rats still had mammalian bodies and I could appreciate my connectedness to them through intercorporeality, a tacit form of intersubjectivity, but because they were not "responsive" to me or to anything, I could not discern any subjective qualities in them. Their intersubjectivity with me was almost totally missing.

That's the sense in which lack of intersubjective activity is a definition of death. It's assessed by intersubjective intuition (which can be wrong). We would like to have a device comparable to Dr. McCoy's tricorder from the television series, *Star Trek*. McCoy would pass his hand-held gadget over a person's body and pronounce "He's dead, Jim." The only intersubjective detector we have is our own self-relating subjectivity. That detector is robust in the mature mind and while fallible at times, nevertheless provides a ready criterion of mental death.

4. What I'm Not

Other people die, not me. I haven't died and don't plan to. I am present to myself. A dead person is intersubjectively absent, even if their body is still present to my senses such as at a funeral or in a hospital. What is lost is the present and future possibility of my intersubjective interaction with that person.

In making that assessment, I exercise my intersubjective faculties. When I acknowledge that the person is dead, I simultaneously assert that I am not. Maybe the other's death makes me wonder if I will be too, soon. Or maybe I reassure myself that death is a long time off for me. It's all about me. A mental definition of being dead is implicitly, "What I am not."

Dead is not merely the *absence* of mentality. We don't say a rock is dead. Rocks presumably lack mentality. But "dead" is a descriptor for a system that once was mentally alive to itself, but now is not. Death implicitly refers to a former state of aliveness.

5. It Tolls for Thee

Another aspect of mental death is the hole left by a person's absence from the social network. When a well-known person dies, eulogies often assert that "we all are diminished by the loss." That is more than poetry. Because we are highly intersubjective, the loss of one member is felt as a loss among the survivors. That's the basis of our grief. We think of persons as individuals but that is only half the story. Each person is a part of a community.

There is no person totally outside any community, even if they think they are, because no one can survive alone. Even a lonely hermit in a mountain cave has education, values, memories, language, mental context, and other living residuals of community life. Part of a mental definition of death is the felt loss among the survivors upon removal of one of the members.

The loss is primarily intersubjective absence, but is larger than that. It also covers the person's social roles, now vacant, and their habitual spaces, tools, artifacts, and resources. Surviving offspring and other relatives become mnemonics for the deceased in the minds of other survivors. There is a "hole" in the network that has the shape of the deceased. That is part of a mental definition of death for the community.

6. Death as a BHN

If death is like other BHNs, the most clear mental definition of death is its lack of experience and self-awareness. We know that from repeated incursions into and out of ordinary BHNs. This definition explicitly does not say anything about the nature of embodiment. It's a purely mental definition. It also doesn't assume anything about the duration of a BHN. Some BHNs last longer than others (in retrospect).

Death, as far as we can tell, lasts a very long time, but based on its equation to ordinary BHNs, it is not, as commonly assumed, a one-way trip. All ordinary BHNs are temporary. We must withhold judgment about the duration of death if we assume it is like other BHNs. Conversely, if death is an ordinary BHN, every ordinary BHN is also a death. It will take some effort to unpack these ideas.

The Process of Dying

If death is a kind of BHN, then difference between alive and dead should be the same as the difference between mentality and a BHN. But the analogy is not perfect because both "alive" and "dead" carry implicit biological connotations. Both life and death are on the biological side of the fence that separates biology from experience. By examining the process of dying, perhaps we can spot a point at which biology and mentality line up in our definition.

Medical Dying

In the days and hours before death, a dying person's language changes. They often talk about the past as if it were the present. Observers notice a dying person's lack of interest about being with family members and friends, even though they still talk about them. The dying person also may stop responding to questions and talk about needing to pack and get ready to take a trip.

As the person dies, bodily functions slow down. As circulation slows, less oxygen reaches the brain and the person often becomes unconscious or sleeps for long periods. Within the twenty-four hours before death, the person sometimes sits up and talks lucidly for a brief spell. Otherwise, a steady decline in responsiveness continues.

The skin becomes gray, mottled, and blotchy as circulation fails. Blood pressure drops. Breathing becomes labored. There may be gasping and periods of no breathing. Eyes become glassy. Hands and feet are cold.

Finally, all respiration stops and the skin becomes cold. No respiration or heartbeat is apparent and the person does not respond to any stimulus. At that point, they have probably died. A flat EEG (brainwave recording) would confirm it.

Experiential Dying

Information about experiential dying comes from people who have "almost died" but then recovered. Since they didn't actually die, we cannot be sure if these reports are complete or accurate.

A dying person often experiences illusions, delusions, and hallucinations. Illusions are misperceptions such as thinking a friend is a deceased family member or that sounds outside the room are from intruders hiding in the room. Delusions are confused beliefs, such as thinking caregivers are trying to harm them. Hallucinations include imagined voices and images that seem real.

Near-death survivors report that hearing is the last sense to terminate and hearing voices in the room persists the longest. When the senses cease operating, the person appears to be in a coma, not responsive. Whether that's because the dying person does not register any sensory input, or just ignores it, or cannot respond to it—we don't know.

Near-death survivors say that despite being unable to respond, they still felt pain and distress. They sensed death approaching and felt they would soon be with deceased loved ones or with God. Sometimes that immanence is represented by a bright light in the distance and the sounds of high-pitched bells. However, near-death survivors turn away from all that and revive, so they cannot report what happens next.

One palliative-care specialist who has watched many people die compares dying to astronomical black holes. "We can see the effect of black holes, but it is extremely difficult, if not impossible, to look inside them. They exert an increasingly strong gravitational pull the closer one gets to them...Most dying people then close their eyes and appear to be asleep. From this point on ... we can only infer what is actually happening." (Dear, 2016).

The *Egyptian Book of the Dead* and the *Tibetan Book of the Dead* are ancient books that mainly describe funerary practices for the living. The Tibetan book does contain descriptions of "what it is like" to die. Presumably, those descriptions came from physicians, near-death survivors, and deep meditators who inferred the process from observations and experience with other BHNs.

According to the *Tibetan Book of the Dead*, the experiential process of dying occurs in six stages, or bardos. A dying person moves sequentially through these stages to finally emerge into a new life, which is the sixth bardo, where we are now.

The Six Bardos of Death

Very briefly, and with apologies to generations of Buddhist scholars, the bardos in the experiential process of dying can be described as:

1. Loss of body awareness and sensation.

2. Bright light and a sense of being in the presence of deities.

3. Sense of being at the center of creation, understanding everything.

4. Collapse of the light into black nothingness.

5. Stirrings of desire, emotion, and discernment.

6. Rebirth into a more enlightened life.

Surprisingly, that summary description maps closely to the experience of yoga meditation when read metaphorically rather than literally.

The first bardo describes the Inward Fold, the willful shutting down of mental self-awareness and bodily senses as one approaches the meditative BHN.

The "bright light" of the second bardo is the metaphorical light of clear understanding that occurs in the meditative BHN. It is unencumbered by bodily, mnemonic, or sensory distractions.

As the meditative BHN draws closer, others are not represented in mind as people but only as a sense of intersubjective connectedness. That sense could fairly be labeled as feeling the presence of "deities."

The third bardo is not consistent with my experience. That may be due to my limited success as a meditator. Certainly there is a profound moment of peace and fullness, but any "understanding" is deferred until emergence from the meditative BHN in the Outward Fold (bardo five).

Bardo #4 denotes entrance into the BHN itself.

Bardo #5 is like coming out of a meditative BHN. In *Scientific Introspection* (Adams, 2020), I called the phenomena of the Fifth Bardo the "Outward Fold," a period prior to full consciousness during which one can intuit the inner structures and operations of the mind itself. It is possible during this period to preliminarily conceptualize ("discern") many phenomena both subjective and objective. It is roughly analogous to the earliest moments of the quasi-awake period during which dreams are fabricated.

"Rebirth," the Sixth Bardo, can be understood as full emergence from the BHN into ordinary experience again. After a BHN, life is never exactly the same as it was before. One has additional knowledge garnered during the Outward Fold, a reconstituted sense of self, a fresh view of the world and one's place in it, and an openness to new instances of intuition and synchronicity. It is a metaphorical rebirth.

In *The Psychedelic Experience* (1964), Metzner, Alpert, and Leary mapped the bardos to their experiences with LSD. Comparing such accounts of metaphysical journeys with written documents like *The Tibetan Book of the Dead* and the *Yoga Sutras*, we can perhaps discern plausible outlines of the experience of dying.

Conclusion:

Comparing the third-person, objective description of dying with what we know of the first-person, experiential process of dying, we see that there are some points of contact. During the experiential process, sensory awareness of the world diminishes, which maps to the observation that a dying person gradually becomes unresponsive to stimulation and apparently uninterested in their surroundings. When the BHN is entered completely (Bardo #4), external observers probably pronounce the person dead.

In the medical process of dying, bardos 5 and 6 do not exist, but then, none of them do, really, because the external point of view cannot directly access any experience. The scientific and medical description of dying truncates at the parallel bardo #4. It's all over at that point from the biological point of view, but not for the mental.

We conclude that biological accounts of death seem to run roughly in parallel with experiential accounts, though with virtually no overlap. We shall proceed as best we can with the experiential descriptions based on findings from examination of non-death BHNs.

Afterlife

Dead is dead. The term "afterlife" is an oxymoron. Despite the obvious absurdity of the concept, it persists and is widely pervasive in human cultures. What explains that?

Partly, the notion of life after death is simply a denial of death as a certainty which few people care to contemplate. But that is such a transparently foolish reaction, it cannot explain the strength of the afterlife idea. Is there a deeper intuition to be had?

The Christian account of afterlife has elements similar to Plato's *Myth of Er* from the Fifth Century, BCE. A soldier named Er dies in battle and is transported to another world. He sees the gates of heaven and hell monitored by judges who evaluate each traveler. He watches the dead drink from the River of Forgetfulness then choose new situations to be reborn to. He is swept by a storm back to the land of the living, where he awakes at his own funeral and tells the tale. That's Plato's description of what happens after death.

Christian doctrine is, roughly, that after death, one is taken into the presence of God to be judged for one's deeds. Depending on the verdict of that trial, one is assigned to heaven or hell for all eternity. The Roman Catholic church has an additional remedial stage, purgatory, in which sinners can be cleansed then sent on to heaven with a good chance of getting in.

It's difficult to find a description of heaven in the *Bible*. Some scholars say references to paradise come from descriptions of ancient Persian gardens. They were the royalty's walled gardens in the desert, oases, cool water surrounded by plants and fresh fruits. The garden of Eden in the *Book of Genesis* might be a description of one of those gardens. While not located anywhere in time or space, a heavenly garden would seem to have spatiotemporal qualities.

If death was only a biological event, it would have little or no import for a spiritual life. That explains religions' minimization of biological death. Instead, religions focus on spiritual life after biological death, though the interface between biology and spirit goes largely undefined. Further, since life and mind as we know them only occur in a body, it is unclear what kind of "life" an unembodied afterlife would be like.

It is impossible to take the idea of afterlife literally, but we can take religious eschatology as a crude expression of the idea that not all of a person is defined by biology. Some part of us is non-biological. That's a more reasonable interpretation of the concept of "afterlife."

Epistemology First

This essay and the others in this series privilege first-person experience over biology because knowledge only arises from experience. Epistemology is the study of what can be known and how. A first-person investigation prioritizes epistemology.

Epistemology asks what can be known with certainty. The only defensible answer, it seems to me, is the presence of the mind itself. If you didn't have that, you couldn't have asked the question. From that start, a secondary question is the role the body plays in the structure and operation of the mind, not the reverse. With a first-person epistemological approach, we do not ask where the mind fits into biology, because it doesn't. We instead ask how the body fits into mentality.

If you start with biology and with science as the only epistemological method, you fairly quickly arrive at a dead-end. You can't get to the mind from the body. The scientific method does not "do" mental objects, only physical ones. The only way to get at the mind is to start with the mind. That's why these essays adopt a first-person point of view.

Naturalism

Another principle of the investigative methodology adopted in these essays has been naturalism. We accept as evidence only natural phenomena (including non-physical ones), empirically observed (including by first-person observational methods), and logical inferences from that. The mind is a natural phenomenon, and introspection, properly defined, is an empirical method of observation.

In a naturalistic approach, we rule out supernatural phenomena and non-empirical evidence. We do not accept the presence or actions of gods and spirits as explanations. Once we do all that, religious accounts of afterlife cease to make any sense.

Within a naturalistic, empirical framework, first-person, empirical epistemology allows us to interrogate the idea that some part of the human person survives biological death. Here's how it could.

How Something Could Survive Death

1. Bodies are Physical, Minds are Not

The mind is non-physical, not defined by time, space, and the laws of physics. Experience is bigger than physics, because physics is a set of descriptions and explanations about certain experiences. Those descriptions are usually presented without reference to the first-person experience that gave rise to them, but that's just a quirk of scientific language.

The nonphysical mind is connected to the physical world in a way we do not understand, but the mind, especially the imagination, often transcends embodiment. These two facts, that experience is larger than physicality, and that mentality can escape physicality, allow scope for consideration of the mind surviving physical death.

2. All BHNs Terminate

The working assumption, or hypothesis if it can be proved, is that death is a kind of BHN, no different in principle from other BHNs. Since all other BHNs eventually terminate to give way to resumed or restarted experience, death must also. That leaves open the possibility that some kind of experience follows death.

3. Minds are Intersubjective

Since the mind is importantly defined by intersubjectivity (Adams, 2021a, 2021b), any one individual mind is a node in a larger network of minds. Since death, as commonly understood, applies to individuals, the social aspects of the mind that are transpersonal, or super-individual, would survive any individual death. That opens a possible avenue though the quasi-mentality of the community to examine communal mental experience of death beyond the experience of any one individual. An example of doing that is reading the *Tibetan Book of the Dead*.

4. Dark Mentality

A close examination of the micro-BHNs that occur in each pulse of the QMP mental cycle reveals the possibility of a modal aspect to mentality. BHNs within ordinary mental activity are a different "mode" or dimension of mentality. They constitute a hypothetical "dark mentality," the "noxperience" of BHN operations. Understanding BHN activity offers the possibility of tracking ordinary experience into noxperience and out the other side of a BHN to experience again.

It is not unreasonable to think that death, as a BHN, might be similarly modal and oscillatory as the micro-BHNs are in the QMP cycle. If that were true, the idea of death as the termination of life would be wrong. Instead, we would have to consider the possibility that death is an ongoing mode of existence that one visits frequently throughout life.

Frequent, oscillatory journeys into death are not remembered because of the extreme disjunction between experience and noxeperience. Nevertheless, from a pseudo-omniscient point of view that conceptualizes both sides, death is a recurring phenomenon within life. That idea provides justification to consider the possibility of life "after" death, or more correctly, life alternating with death throughout the objectively-assessed "lifespan."

Post-death Mentality

In sum then, the conventional view of an afterlife is self-contradictory and even unintelligible. However, we still should retain the idea that some kind of mentality could follow death—probably not a personal kind of mentality, but some kind. The idea of death as a terminus could be wrong.

Oblivion Reconsidered

Once we have reason to assert that some part of a person survives death, we can find arguments against the opposite, that death results in utter personal oblivion. Here are some reasons to question the thesis of complete and permanent mental oblivion at death:

1. Elements might survive.

The material elements of a person's body survive death due to the principle of conservation of matter and energy. One's body is recycled into atoms and heat to be re-used elsewhere in the great churn of change. Mentality is not physical, but it is legitimate to wonder if any elements of it survive death as the elements of the body do.

2. Oblivion is Undefined

Future oblivion is an incoherent proposition. We do not predict future experience well, and that includes prediction of future non-experience. We have no experiential history from which to predict eternal personal oblivion. Moreover, if the assertion of oblivion is true, then after death there would be no entity to stand in relationship to non-self-existence, making the assertion of oblivion empty of meaning. Since only a living person can propose oblivion, the most one can properly say is that one's ontological status after death is unknown.

3. Mentality is Social

One's mentality is socially constructed in collaboration with one's community. An individual cannot alone suffer oblivion because individuality is actually a compound of self and intersubjective others. The most one can properly say is that after death, self-awareness of individuality would not prevail. Other, intersubjective aspects of mentality could persist. For example, we remember the dead. Each person persists as a mnemonic trace in the ongoing community of survivors. Utter oblivion is not a fact of communal experience.

4. Oblivion is Posited only by the Living

Oblivion at death is defined from an imagined future first-person point of view, but we, the alive community, discussing this matter now, are not compelled to take that point of view. We are a collaboration of individuals. As a community we do not perish when one individual does. Oblivion is therefore an entirely imagined construct with no basis in experience.

5. Oblivion is Egocentric Delusion

Commonsense says you're born alone and you die alone. Neither of those is true. In particular, you cannot die alone because people are not monads. Each individual consciousness extends into a web of intersubjective influence. The proposition that your individuality suffers oblivion at death is an egocentric delusion, like a leaf saying the tree must perish when the leaf turns yellow. The assertion of personal oblivion is based on a narrow, first-person conception of "the personal."

6. Fact is Consensus

Only the consensus community validates what is true and what is not. There is no criterion of truth beyond that. (Of course, consensus does not mean unamimity). What individuals believe to be true is derived from their consensus community. All personal beliefs, therefore, are communally constructed and historically contingent, including a belief in personal oblivion at death. Therefore it is only possible to suggest personal oblivion upon death on a contingent basis. It cannot be taken as an ontological fact.

Conclusion

Death, commonly understood, is the termination of life, a one-time-only event. Few people are pleased with that prospect so the possibility that death is not final has arisen in human culture going back as far as history. In some versions, one lives again in heaven, while in others, one lives again on Earth. None of those ideas makes logical sense. The very idea of "life after death" is self-contradictory if death means the end of life.

However, if we re-frame death, the situation looks different. The first-person, experiential point of view does not begin with the fact of biology. It begins with the fact of self-awareness. Death then can be recast from the point of view of experience as a kind of BHN, a Black Hole of Nothingness, not different in principle from other known BHNs.

In that case, when we compare what we know about other BHNs to the BHN of death, we find good reasons to think that death is not best defined as the termination of experience. Rather, we see openings for continued experiential persistence "on the other side" of death. What that persistence is, we cannot say at this point, but the possibility gives us impetus to explore further.

The Soul

Before we move on, we need to dispense with the notion of the soul. In most religions and throughout literature and history, it is "the soul" that persists across death. We should, with respect, take a moment to consider what that means, and see if there is anything useful to be gleaned from that idea.

History of The Soul

The soul is supposedly the immaterial spiritual and vital part of a person. Animals may or may not have souls, depending on who you talk to. In theology, the soul is that part of the person that partakes of divinity. Most importantly, all definitions of it insist that the soul is immortal. Since the body is clearly not immortal, that means the soul continues after a person's death.

It hardly seems necessary to note that there is no scientific evidence for the existence of a soul. Some early investigators attempted to detect one by watching for escaping waves or vapors at the moment of death. None were ever seen. Others have meticulously weighed bodies immediately before and immediately after death to see if there was a difference. No such study has ever caught a soul in the act of escaping.

There is no physical, perceptual, or instrumental evidence for a soul, but is there a logical necessity to assert its existence? Many definitions of soul implicitly equate it with a vital spirit. Whatever it is that makes you alive rather than dead is what the soul is.

Since we do not have a good scientific definition of "alive," invoking a vital principle can be a substitute definition for a soul. We need something to explain why people are alive and corpses are not. However, vitality does not, by definition, survive death, so equating the soul to a vital principle doesn't really get you anything.

Other definitions of soul compare it or equate it with creativity, optimism, empathy, personality, or understanding: almost any psychological trait. Psychological traits and mental characteristics are considered to be non-material, and that makes them distinct and separate from the material body. Could they be the soul? Anything's possible when it comes to souls, but there's no logical necessity to suppose that one's mind and personality survive death and plenty of evidence from BHNs that they don't. So soul as personality doesn't work very well.

Kinds of Soul

For the ancient Egyptians, breath was the vital principle, but they defined two kinds of breath. One stayed with the body and died with it, but the other kind was immortal and followed the deceased to the land of the dead.

Why a dead person without a body would need to breathe was not explained. Perhaps the practice of mummification was designed to partially address that issue. Though mummies do not breathe, at least they had lungs.

The ancient Chinese, like the Egyptians, specified a two-part soul. There was a bodily soul like a vital principle which perished at death, and a higher, immortal soul which was abstract and cognitive. The immortal component had to be cognitive to facilitate ancestor-worship. What good would it do to pray to your ancestors if they couldn't understand you? The ancestors needed lively minds. The immortal soul was therefore similar to the cognitive description of the living mind, making communication with the ancestors possible.

In ancient Greek, the term *psyche* meant both soul and breath. That allowed discrimination of the soul's immateriality from its immortality. However, Pythagoras, a pre-Socratic, dispensed with the vital principle. He said the soul was only the immortal part, a spark of divinity. It exists before birth, during life, and after death. Breath had nothing to do with it.

Socrates, Plato, and Aristotle agreed that the soul had a divine nature, and said it was also capable of reasoning and logic because those are divine faculties. Even after death therefore, you were able to think. That was useful for Plato, who believed in reincarnation.

Reincarnation puts a lot of demands on the soul. The soul has to survive loss of the body at death, serve as the ongoing spiritual and cognitive principle, and become re-animated repeatedly in new bodies. Plato met these requirements by specifying a three-part soul. It was made of *logos*, the rational mind; *thymos*, the emotional spirits; and *eros*, desire, or motivation in general.

Aristotle, ever the troublemaker, said okay but only the logos part is immortal. The other two aspects of the soul were merely vital principles and they died with the body. The logos however, had to be immortal because it had the characteristic of being self-conscious. You need rationality to be self-aware. Without that, you'd be absolutely nowhere after you died.

Early Christianity adopted Aristotle's view, adding the rule that God creates each individual soul at the moment of conception. That guaranteed that the immortal soul was more than just a principle of self-awareness or a rational faculty. It was also divine.

Later, Aquinas changed the formula again to recapture the essence of Plato's three-part plan. The intellectual part, the logos, *included* the other two parts, he said. That meant all three parts of the soul, intellect, emotion, and motivation, were divine and "incorruptible." While the body perishes at death, motivation and emotion could survive along with the intellect or logos.

Since reincarnation was no longer part of Christianity at that time (the 1200s), having a complete, functioning mind in heaven, with intellect, motivation and emotion, was necessary, considering that you would spend all eternity there. Eternal life would be no fun at all with a rational faculty but no motivation or emotion to go with it.

Christian thinking about the soul continued to evolve. Some groups (Calvinists, Lutherans, Jehovah's Witnesses), said that at death, the soul becomes dormant, but then "comes back to life" with resurrection into heaven. That assured that ghosts don't have a soul because they don't resurrect.

Hindu traditions defined the soul as the divine spiritual essence of a person but divided it into two parts, the individual soul and the universal soul. Those two are separated at birth, and the aim of life is to get them reunited. Some Vedantic texts say they aren't really divided, you just think they are. In reality, the Atman, or individual soul, is identical with the transcendent Brahman. Your job is to get un-confused about that.

In Shamanism, common in many pre-industrial societies even today, humans have two distinct souls. The body-soul provides vitality while a free-soul disconnects from the body and wanders in the spirit world during sleep and in trance states. If the free-soul does not get back to the body in a timely manner, the person becomes sick or goes insane. The shaman's healing role is to travel into the spirit world, find the AWOL free-soul and bring it back. That cures the sick person.

In Theosophy, a nineteenth-century blend of Eastern and Western religious ideas, the soul encompasses vital body functions and mental faculties but, as in Shamanism, also involves out-of-body phenomena such as astral travel.

In sharp contrast, Buddhists have no soul. There is a cycle of death and birth but it isn't personal. Your so-called inner self or divine soul is illusory. However, as Buddhism does endorse reincarnation, logically there must be, if not a soul, some other element that persists beyond death. Otherwise, reincarnation would not make sense. The persistent element is not clearly specified in Buddhism (as far as my understanding goes).

Ghosts

A word should be given to ghosts since they have featured prominently in traditions and arts around the world. Ghosts range from mindless screaming banshees to articulate and helpful informants like the ghost of Hamlet's father. Many traditions describe them as the un-reborn dead trudging through the post-life bardos where they wander without purpose. Their "lifespan" (an odd concept for a ghost) is forty-nine days, according to *The Tibetan Book of the Dead*.

What do ghosts want? Supposedly, they want to get out of the post-death bardo like everybody else, but they can't. They are stuck, unable to "let go" of their former life. They have detachment disorder. Ghosts who seek revenge on the living, a solid trope of horror stories, are particularly attached to life. As far as we know, there are no ghost psychologists to help them work through their issues and move on—clearly a business opportunity lost.

Ghosts have bodies, sort of. An unembodied person is unimaginable to us. At the same time, the body of the deceased is visibly dead, so that's useless. Consequently, ghosts find a compromise, a quasi-body, a pale, wavering, semi-transparent ghost-body.

The ancient Egyptians provided not just bodies but massive houses (pyramid tombs) with food, weapons, vehicles, money, and slaves for the dead, everything they would need "on the other side." Many historical and prehistorical cultures buried elaborate provisions with the dead to aid with expected tribulations in the afterlife.

Perhaps the interface between decomposing bodies and funerary goods and the spirit-world was not well-thought-out, but it expressed the fact that we are confused about what continues after death and our cultural images of ghosts demonstrate that.

Conclusion

There are no ghosts, I'm sorry to say—sorry because I've written several novels featuring them (e.g., Adams 2023b). But the idea of ghosts is interesting for what it reveals about cultural ideas concerning death and the persistence of some personal element beyond death.

That persistent personal element is not the soul because there is no soul. If I'm wrong, well, too bad for me.

Cultural ideas about the soul are not coherent enough to extract useful ideas. At best, they reinforce the idea that some aspects of personal experience are non-material and could, in principle, persist across death. The supposed divine aspect of the soul is out of scope for this essay, which does not consider supernatural phenomena. But non-divine aspects of the non-material body could conceivably survive death.

What could those be? We take up that question next.

What Persists across a BHN

Two micro-BHNs inhabit the QMP cycle. While each temporarily stops it, mentality always restarts. After it does, self and world seem much as they were before, giving rise to the illusion of a continuous stream of consciousness. The only way that could happen is if some aspect of mental experience survived both BHNs. We want to know what can survive nothingness.

One approach to the problem is to rule out what does *not* survive a BHN. We can do that from analysis of the BHN. BHNs "contain" no experience, by definition, but careful examination of them, as was done in *Nothing in Mind*, (Adams, 2023a), tells us about what disappears upon entering a BHN.

What is Lost On Entry Into a BHN

The tripartite modular mind evaporates. The motivational IMS, the bodily SMC and the thinking SLM all disappear. Entering the meditative BHN explicitly minimizes each module until the last one, the SLM, finally blinks out. Less willfully, much the same thing happens when falling asleep. No aspect of the ordinary mind survives entry into a BHN.

No Body

The body, including the brain are absent in a BHN. No personal point of view remains from which to say that the body persists.

No World

The world, its history, and all its people evaporate. As with the body, all experience of the world is lost upon entry into a BHN.

No Self

The personal self dissipates. A personality, a sense of "me," an ego with a point of view—none of those survives entry into a BHN.

No Awareness

All self-awareness is lost, even the implicit sense of self-existence that one has in a dream.

No Memory

No memories of self, other, body or world survive in a BHN. No new memories are formed either because there is nothing to remember. Nor is the fact of nothingness experienced or remembered.

No Emotions

Emotions and feelings do not survive entry into a BHN.

No Intersubjective Relationships

Relationships with other people do not survive, not even implicitly as they do in a dream.

Implications

When we apply that list to death, which is just a great-big BHN, we see a few interesting implications:

1. There is no aspect of ordinary mentality that survives death, so if a soul persists, it is incapable of thought, feeling, or understanding. Prayers and ancestor worship would be wasted on such a soul.

2. If there is a heaven or other divine domain, it would be devoid of all experience, thoughts, feelings, communications, and relationships. It could only be a domain of nothingness and non-experience.

3. There is no possibility of reunification with loved ones after death. If remnants of formerly deceased people were somehow present after death, they would be unknown and unknowable to the person who just died. Communication with them would be impossible in principle.

4. The deceased cannot communicate with or even be aware of living survivors. A dead person cannot "look down on" or "watch over" any living person because all self-aware links to other people are lost upon entry into a BHN. There are no "guardian angels."

Those are just some of the applications of evidence we have from ordinary BHNs. We would need additional evidence to support any contrary claims about death.

Despite a long list of losses, absences, and impossibilities associated with entrance into a BHN, we know that something must persist. We know that because upon emergence from an ordinary BHN, the world and the mind that beholds it seem to continue as if uninterrupted. That would not be possible if everything were totally and permanently obliterated with entry into a BHN. Something survives. What is it?

A Wrong Answer

The easy but wrong answer to the question of what persists is that the world continues during a BHN but the mind doesn't know it. That answer says that upon emergence, or "awakening," from the BHN, the mind simply becomes aware again of what was there the whole time. We should resist that seductive answer. It involves a host of errors and contradictions.

The main difficulty is that the easy answer is no answer at all. Saying that "the mind becomes aware again" is an astonishing statement. How could it? Why should it? Nothing comes from nothing.

An embedded assumption in the easy answer is that the brain, or something else in the world, *causes* the mind to appear and disappear. Maybe neurological activity does the trick or synaptic biochemistry. But any explanation like that makes the mind epiphenomenal, a non-causal byproduct of brain activity like the exhaust emitted from a car's tailpipe.

Yet if the mind is merely a waste product of the brain, then this explanation is meaningless. Brains cannot appreciate meaning any more than stones can. The easy answer would be self-refuting if it carried any meaning, but it doesn't because it can't.

Yet another formidable problem with the "persistent world" explanation is that from the first-person, or experiential point of view, the world patently does *not* persist through a BHN. The "N" in BHN means Nothingness. To assert that the world persists through a BHN is a denial of the experience we are trying to explain.

Third-person Point of View

If one adopts a third-person, public point of view then yes, the world and the body persist continuously over time. That's the observational fact. But in that point of view, there is no such thing as a BHN. Minds are only known from first-person observation (introspection).

First-person Point of View

From the first-person (subjective) point of view, there is no legitimate ground to say that the world persists over a BHN. To jump surreptitiously from first- to third-person points of view in an unprincipled way is a category error, an error in reasoning.

Memory

The first-person point of view supports the idea of memory, which the third person point of view does not. (Third-person "objective" memory is functional memory, not phenomenological memory. More on that later.)However, we must resist the commonplace explanation of world-persistence across a BHN. What's a better explanation? It can't be traditional memory.

Earlier, I argued that the traditional idea storage-and-retrieval memory cannot be correct, but that a kind of reconstructive memory makes sense. But if memory is a reconstruction, it needs a seed from which to germinate. You can't construct, or reconstruct something from nothing. So what is the seed?

The Three Seeds

We suppose that some mental element must persist across the nothingness of a BHN. If a BHN entailed complete and permanent obliteration of all mentality, nothing mental would ever happen again. That is a possible definition of death, but for all other BHNs, something must persist. All we have to do is identify the persistent seed. Close analysis reveals more than one.

Study of repeated BHNs over a long period of time produced the following seed candidates:

1. Commodity Subjectivity
2. The Planck Code
3. The Motivating Force

Here's the derivation of that list:

Commodity Subjectivity

Imagine a non-personal, un-individuated kind of subjectivity that survives the BHN. Call it "commodity subjectivity."

Commodity Subjectivity is not my subjectivity, not your subjectivity, not anybody's subjectivity. It is a non-personal, non-individual, undifferentiated commodity, like cookie dough in the bowl before it is rolled out and cut into cookies. Cookie-dough subjectivity is not sufficient to function in a mind. It is not self-relating subjectivity, and it is not an element of mentality. Simondon (cited by Grosz, 2017 and by Combes, 2013) identifies this generic state of subjectivity as "the pre-individual."

Mentality requires a bounded, individual instance of subjectivity, as shown in the diagram of QMP mentality (Figure

49

1). That's the SRS, the kind of subjectivity that makes up the subjective component of a particular mind. Mental SRS is proto-self-aware, and is also, by implication, tacitly proto-aware of whatever is not itself.

Commodity Subjectivity, by contrast, is a basic subjective "substance" that does not support mentality. SRS is variant of Commodity Subjectivity that occurs outside the BHN. Commodity Subjectivity itself lies within the domain of the BHN where there is no mentality.

The Planck Code

The second element that survives the BHN is information about the experiential world left behind. Without that, a new mentality would start an entirely new life in an entirely new world. That does not correspond to our experience, which seems continuous over BHNs.

Imagine a kernel of information called the Planck Code as a nexus of information that persists over the BHN, connecting pre- and post-BHN experience in ordinary mentality. The Planck Code is a compressed information pattern made up of essential invariants of experience sufficient to reconstruct a recognizable post-BHN world of experience. It "resides" in the BHN, and so does not participate in the QMP cycle of mentality.

We might think of the Planck Code as a bar code. It contains information, not much, but enough. When a scanner reads a bar code and connects it to an appropriate system, a complete data set can be recovered.

Another analogy is the DNA double helix. Simple though it is, it contains the essential information that various kinds of RNA can read to create full, complex, folded proteins and ultimately, the body plan for an entire animal.

The important thing about the Planck Code is that it's not personal. Nothing personal survives a BHN. The Planck Code is information about a *kind* of life, regardless of whose life it is. It encodes relatively invariant qualities of intersubjective relationships between an individual and their community over a lifespan. The Planck Code does not encode a person's experience, but derivative qualities of that experience.

The Planck Code's information is like the bar code for bananas. It doesn't specify any particular banana. Generic information is enough to build a particular life pattern in a post-BHN world.

The Motivating Force

Whatever survives a BHN needs animation to accomplish the reconstruction of self and world on the outward side. That motivation is the "fuel" that gets the new self and world going again after the BHN. If there were no such fuel, a BHN would be forever. Sleep would be fatal.

The Motivating Force is goal-oriented, as opposed to being an explosion of energy in a random direction or in all directions. The Motivating Force can be imagined as an arrow with a pointed end and a tail end. The anchors are Commodity Subjectivity and the Planck Code. The Motivating Force animates their interaction, which is sufficient to rebuild the world after the BHN.

The Motivating Force is not personal. It is a commodity motivation that energizes the field of Commodity Subjectivity. That's why it's called a "force" rather than any named personal motive. The Motivating Force operates within the domain of the BHN itself, not in the domain of ordinary mentality.

Enduring a BHN

We now have a list of three elements that putatively survive any BHN, as assessed retrospectively by a post-BHN mind. These elements are sufficient to create a convincing post-BHN world, including the QMP architecture of mind itself and all the contents of experience, current and remembered, that make up the first-person mental world.

How do these three elements manage to do that? The answer will take some time to explain, but in brief: these elements are already in the BHN. They are like its cellular cytoplasm, what a BHN is made of. They become customized to form individuated self-relating subjectivity, mental intentionality, and personal experience outside the BHN.

That's the high level view of why experience seems continuous across BHNs. These three elements tie the pre- and post- BHN experiences together. They are the persistent seeds of the reconstruction.

Before jumping into how the post-BHN reconstruction works in detail, we need to better understand one of the persistent elements of continuous experience, the Planck Code.

The Planck Code

The Planck Code is one of the seeds that survives the nothingness of a BHN. It can be thought of as the intersection of an individual's life with their contextual community across moments of intersubjective engagement.

Such moments happen during teaching and learning, love and loss, talk and gesture, understanding and social intuition. Those are some of the ways we interact with each other. Social interactions begin during gestation and continue throughout life. It's how we live and it's from intersubjective encounters that we construe self and world.

Lifelong intersubjective interaction is composed of millions or billions of events, but that's not what's stored in the Planck Code. It's not a record of events. Rather, the Planck Code is a characterization of the overall style and trend of interaction, the *quality* of intersubjectivity over time.

The number of interactive styles people engage in is large but finite. We might approximate some of those characteristics with reference to psychological traits from personality theory. Traits are theoretical constructs that summarize a person's temperament, interests, abilities, and style of social interaction over millions of events in a lifespan. Such persistent traits transcend any one individual interaction.

Personality Traits

A prominent example is the list of traits known as The Big Five (Fiske, 1949). Each trait is measured on a scale from one anchor to its opposite, like introversion-extraversion. A person can be characterized as somewhere between the extremes. With scores on each of the five traits, the person has a characteristic "profile."

The five "Big" traits with defining endpoints are:

Openness: Curious, open to change and imaginative; versus the opposite: inflexible, traditional and predictable.

Conscientiousness: Self-disciplined, organized, and thoughtful; versus the complement, such as impulsive, disorganized, careless.

Extraversion: Sociable, outgoing, seeking excitement; versus introversion: reflective, reserved, seeking privacy.

Agreeableness: Trusting, altruistic, cooperative; versus suspicious, manipulative, antagonistic.

Neuroticism: Anxious, shy and moody; versus calm, confident and emotionally steady.

The Five-Factor rubric is an example. I am not saying that the Planck Code is a personality index. I am not even saying that the Big Five traits are real intrinsic traits of a person. There are many theoretical problems with this list and with any such system of traits.

The Big Five is presented here just an example of abstract, meta-qualities of a person's interactive style that can be conceptualized, measured and labeled. The traits supposedly represent the *quality* of the person's interactions over extended time. As meta-data, the trait profile is rather impersonal. It is no longer descriptive of any particular experience. It is at best, quasi-personal.

A Different Example

Another way to conceptualize what's in a Planck Code is by analogy to the various quantum states of an electron. All electrons are identical because they have the exact same mass and charge. Yet any particular electron in context, in a hydrogen atom, for example, is characterized by a unique set of quantum numbers. One, designated n, indexes the electron's energy level, which can be one of three states. The electron's angular momentum, l (the letter L), describes the shape of its unique distribution around the hydrogen nucleus. The electron's magnetic field, m, describes how it orients in space when it's near other atoms. The particular angle of its magnetic moment is its spin, s.

The set of four quantum numbers characterizes any particular electron. If electrons didn't have unique values for n, l, m, and s, chemistry would not be possible because all electrons are identical and they would have no "need" or ability to interact with each other to form molecules and the materials of everyday life. Because they differ in these values, they combine to compensate deficiencies for surpluses, and the reverse, creating molecules.

The electrons' quantum numbers and their range of possible values are examples of the kinds of information that could be stored in a Planck Code. I offer this second example of what a Planck Code might contain because the urge to think that the Planck Code is literally a set of personality traits is hard to resist, but wrong. The Planck Code is a set of parameters for intersubjectivity that in combination, distinguish each person from others. It's what keeps us all from being identical. It's what makes us willing and able to interact. Exactly what constitutes our human parameters of uniqueness is yet unknown.

Personal traits show up when we interact with others, either in real time, or in imagination and memory. For the Planck Code, we also need a set of parameters to characterize kinds of communities, from pre-industrial hunters to space-station astronauts. I don't have an example of such a measurement tool, but I'm sure there are some, and others could be invented.

With a little matrix multiplication, we could then generate a set of data that described every possible quality of interaction between an individual and their community. We could summarize and integrate such data over the span of a lifetime as the interactions occur. It would be a large dataset but finite.

Nobody is Unique

We like to believe every person is "special," but that is not statistically plausible. It's not even true that every snowflake is unique. While the variance is large among measured traits for individuals and communities, it is not infinite.

People are much more the same than they are different. That is true for human bodies and human genetics and for human minds. It is also true for the qualities of intersubjective communities. So it is reasonable to assume that one could usefully capture a running characterization of any person's intersubjective life in a Planck Code pattern.

Characteristic Profiles

Psychological assessment specialists can quickly characterize people into categories with a measurement schema. For example, with MMPI results (Minnesota Multiphasic Personality Inventory: Hathaway and McKinley, 1943), lists of well-defined "profiles" are available. Many people sort neatly into one or more of those categories.

A clinician might say to another MMPI expert, "My patient is a 2-3-7." That means the person is passive-aggressive and has phobias and sexual dysfunction. It's a common pattern. The other clinician would nod knowingly. Again, everyone's different, but not infinitely so. There are types.

An Impersonally Personal Index

The Planck Code captures, in a personally impersonal way, the quality of a life lived. It's a theoretical construct, an abstraction for an accounting of BHN dynamics.

There are a finite number of ways to be with other people. Your way is one of them, but it's not totally unique because you are not totally unique.

The Planck Code is thus quasi-personal, the way that selecting a small, medium, or large tee-shirt is a personal selection. It's customized to your body size and shape, but it's hardly tailor-made. The Planck Code can be "unpacked" upon exit from the BHN as the basis for a newly-constructed intersubjective self and world that you would recognize.

With that basic concept of the Planck Code, let's look more closely at its details.

Definition of the Planck Code

The Planck Code is a theoretical construct for descriptors of a person's main modes or styles of intersubjective interaction. We used the scales of psychological assessment instruments as examples of styles of interaction We can imagine such descriptive information as a dataset.

Why "Planck?"

A Planck star is a hypothetical object at the center of an astronomical black hole (Rovelli, 2014). It is so compact that its energy density reaches the Planck constant where spacetime becomes quantized. That's the smallest possible unit of spacetime. The black hole cannot collapse any more than that, which means it cannot become a singularity. The Planck star thus lets the black hole resist utter oblivion.

I take that cosmological theory as a an apt metaphor for the Planck Code that persists across the mental Black Hole of Nothingness. The Planck Code is something that survives nothing.

We're not literally worried about physical "collapse" or even data storage in the BHN, as mentality does not occur in space and the mind is not really computational. "Planck Code" is just a useful metaphor for a psychological gizmo. One reaches for images from the zeitgeist.

In this deployment of the metaphor, the Planck Code functions as the cumulative, composite record of a life's worth of intersubjective interactions. It stores only essential features consolidated into a mnemonic "seed" that survives a BHN. That seed contains enough information to rebuild a recognizable social world when the BHN is over.

What the Planck Code is For

Life is social for us and a person's social (intersubjective) experience is the experiential information that must survive the BHN. Current culture emphasizes individualism in which each person has a mind with unique private knowledge, feelings, and awareness. That's a practical image for getting many things done, but it's fundamentally inadequate. We are only partially individual. The greater part of us is intersubjective.

What we prize as our individual mind was given to us by the social community through a long process of socialization. We got *everything* socially: language, knowledge, ways of thinking, beliefs, understanding of the world, other people, habits, and culture. Even our "private" thoughts are socially derived from tacit social assumptions, social memories, communal experience and shared language. The physical body is also social. It was given to us by parents. Everything about us is social.

Social means interactive. There is no such thing as a non-social person, because even one's "private" mind and body schema are internalizations and representations of a social context. That's why the Planck Code is a composite of one's social interactions. Information about intersubjective interactions is the most fundamental data we need to rebuild the world as it was before the BHN.

How the Planck Code is Formed and Updated

The Planck Code is a theoretical construct, an abstract mental "device," like Chomsky's "Language Acquisition Device." It's not literally a computational product or device. In this metaphor, it is a continuously updating process that consolidates intersubjective experience. It is not a record of experience. It is more like your online search history, a record of the sites you visited, but not what you saw or did there. It's a record of what you wanted, not a record of what happened.

The Planck Code is updated twice in every mental cycle. Every mental event is defined by the QMP process, the archetypal mental cycle. In each QMP, two BHNs occur, and the Planck Code is updated inside those BHNs. That could be the main reason for those BHNs in the QMP cycle. A BHN might have other functions but it seems likely that one of them is to update the Planck Code during each experience.

No introspection is possible within a BHN for obvious reasons. So, how do I know about the Planck Code? I learned of it indirectly, the way astronomers infer qualities of a cosmological black hole from study of its event horizon. The methodology for study of psychological black holes, or BHNs, is described in Adams (2023a).

Sleep and the Planck Code

Dreamless sleep is one of the larger BHNs in terms of implicit duration. We spend 75% of our nightly sleep time in NREM (Carskadon and Dement, 2005, 2011). Some dreaming and fragmentary cognition occur during NREM periods, but for the most part, we are largely not present to ourselves during NREM sleep. Mentally, we are non-existent, evaporated into a BHN. What goes on during that "time" (as clocked by outside observers)?

Sleep researchers have determined that the body repairs itself during NREM sleep (Tamaki, et al., 2020). Bone and muscle tissue are repaired and grown, the immune system is reset, and various metabolic hormones are rebalanced. Neurological connections are pruned and strengthened.

And apparently, you can't skip it. Sleep deprivation produces increased anxiety, depression, and can even produce mental effects similar to psychosis (NHLBI, 2022). NREM sleep is not optional. Our nightly BHN seems to be necessary for development and maintenance of the body.

The Planck Code is updated during NREM sleep with information that supports awareness of embodiment. Upon exiting the BHN or NREM period, you are more able to reconstitute your familiar embodiment. If you skip sleep, or don't get enough of it, you wake up "groggy," with details of the world and yourself unclear to you. If your body "schema" (to use Merleau-Ponty's term), is not routinely refreshed, you can even feel alienated from your own body.

The other main kind of sleep is REM sleep, during which most dreaming is stimulated. During that part of sleep, the brain is quite active, almost as much as when awake. During dream-formation, we are "sort of" present to ourself. In a dream, we do have awareness of ourself and of others, though that self and world and those relationships are often unlike normal waking experience.

REM sleep is so biologically active (brain and whole body), that it can be considered to be an early stage of the Outward Fold, the transitional period out of a BHN. It is during the Outward Fold, when one is closest to being awake, that dreams are formed. The reconstitution of the world occurs in the Outward Fold, after the BHN. Dreaming is therefore a glimpse into the earliest stages of the world being reconstructed.

During all but the last REM period of the night, a person typically cycles back into NREM sleep without waking up and without reporting any dream. NREM (a BHN) again destroys whatever world-reconstruction might have begun. The last REM period however, continues into full wakefulness. In that case, the journey through the Outward Fold results in full expansion of time and full recovery of normal cognition where the familiar self and world are present.

As with NREM, REM sleep is not optional. Scientists have deprived people of only REM sleep. Whenever the sleeper's brain activity starts to show the characteristic pattern of REM, the scientists awaken the person. After some minutes, the person is allowed to fall again into NREM sleep. But as soon as they show signs of REM, the bell rings again. It sounds cruel, but the results are interesting.

People deprived only of REM sleep show, during wakefulness, symptoms of severe sleep deprivation which can be similar to schizophrenia and bipolar disorder. Even though the person got 75% of a "good night's sleep" in terms of hours of sleeping, the lack of those REM periods results in severe sleep deprivation with associated mental disturbances.

When allowed to sleep normally again, those individuals engage in an unusually large number of prolonged REM periods as if to "make up" for the REM time they missed (Vogel, 1975). So, apparently, not only is REM sleep necessary, we need some fixed amount of it in each diurnal cycle.

One way to interpret that result is to say that rebuilding a whole new self and world after a BHN is difficult. The resources needed for it may be generated during the biological maintenance activity of NREM, when the Planck Code is updated. The actual reconstruction then can proceed in the REM, the Outward Fold. We can observe the early stages of the construction when we remember a dream.

It is during the critical REM periods that the Planck Code is "read out" to support reconstruction of the world one recognizes. If the reading of the Planck Code is disrupted, you get a fragmented, disoriented, unpleasant world, not the one you expected. The severe-sleep-deprived world can be indistinguishable from the world of psychosis.

With this examination of sleep as one of the more accessible BHNs, we can infer that some kinds of sleep (NREM) are very much "lights out" Black Holes of Nothingness, while the REM phase, especially the last one that merges into wakefulness, corresponds to the Outward Fold of a BHN. Examining a dream counts as observing the early stages of reconstruction of the world after the oblivion of the BHN. Details of this interpretation of dreaming are in Adams (2023a).

Why the Planck Code is Not a Memory

The Planck Code shepherds essential information through the oblivion of a BHN so that self and world can be rebuilt on the other side. But that does not make the Planck Code a memory function, at least not a phenomenological memory. Here's why:

No agency executes the Planck Code. No homunculus is responsible for Planck Code formation. Personhood is lost on entry into a BHN. Updating of the Planck code is a passive, functional process, like a stream "updating" a pond by filling it or like each season's tree rings adding to the history of the tree. The update is non-intentional.

A Planck Code carries subjective, not objective information. Its data arise from self-relating subjectivity, specifically inter-subjectivity. In contrast, traditional storage-and-retrieval memory involves objects and events, not subjects. The Planck Code information is not objectified and is therefore inaccessible in principle to any mnemonic retrieval.

The Planck Code is lossy with respect to detail. By analogy, factors are lost to the product when two numbers are multiplied: "30" could have arisen from 5x6 or 10x3. There is no way to know from examination of the product. A Planck Code likewise contains no information about particular experienced objects, events, interactions, or procedures. It does not have the kind of information memory retrieval would need for autobiographical recall.

It hardly needs mentioning, but the Planck Code is not an engram or other biological trace of experience. Subjectively, experientially, and phenomenologically, the body is lost upon entering a BHN. It is not possible that the Planck Code is any kind of biological trace.

The Planck Code does operate like a *functional* memory however. Functional memory is structural resilience. For example, a memory-foam mattress reconstitutes its structural shape after deformation. But there is "nothing it is like" for the mattress to do that. No subjectivity is involved and it is not a real memory. The product is mis-named.

The Planck Code is a nonphysical functional trace of intersubjective interactions. Like a memory foam mattress, intersubjective traces can be changed and yet recover much of their original configuration, a Planck Code retains its configuration between updates. But as with any functional memory, it has no phenomenology.

Death and the Planck Code

Now we can bring discussion of the Planck Code back into the larger problematic, exploring death as a kind of BHN. Throughout this essay, we have assumed that all BHNs work essentially the same way, including death.

The one exception is that, as far as we know, death lasts "forever," whereas all other known BHNs eventually run their course and terminate. Non-death BHNs endure (as assessed in retrospect) for microseconds within the QMP mental cycle, to fractions of an hour for NREM sleep and the meditative BHN. Death is anomalous in its finality. Unless we have mis-conceptualized it.

If we seriously entertain the hypothesis that death is no different from other BHNs, we must consider if death is a state of mind (no-mind) that eventually self-terminates. Under the BHN hypothesis, after death we would expect a termination of the state, followed by a reconstruction of mind and world.

Another implication is that the operation of the Planck Code looks similar to traditional ideas of karma. I'm going to pause to investigate that striking similarity before moving on to compare death and non-death BHNs.

Karma and the Planck code

According to several myths and widespread belief, one of the first things that "happens" after you die is an assessment of your accumulated virtue in life. In Plato's *Myth of Er*, a panel of judges pronounced verdicts on each traveler in the land of the dead. In Christianity, one is judged by God, or possibly by Saint Peter, who guards the Pearly Gates into heaven, according to the *Book of Revelations*.

The doctrine of karma, from Buddhism, Hinduism, Jainism, and other religious traditions, is also a post-life evaluation, but unlike the Abrahamic religions, the judgment is not personified. Karma is like an arithmetic tally of virtue points earned throughout life. One's fate is determined somewhat algorithmically, with no shame or blame.

The karmic evaluation is not intersubjective but impersonally personal. It is often called the "Law of Karma" to emphasize that it is an objective determination, not Santa Claus's opinion about whether you've been "bad or good." It is not even the all-knowing judgment of God or his saints. Karmic evaluation is not personal; it's the law. Nobody judges you.

What is Karma?

Karma is virtue, according to most ancient and modern descriptions. That doesn't quite answer the question, though. What is virtue? In Plato's *Meno*, Socrates struggled to find a definition. Our intuition tells us that virtue is "good." One wants to be virtuous. "Bad" people lack virtue.

The connotations tell us that karma is valenced, positive or negative, like electric charge and magnetism. There is "good karma" and "bad karma."

What makes an action virtuous? We can make a list of virtuous actions from traditional sources and see what they have in common. From that, it looks like virtue accrues from intersubjective activity. The more a person is connected to others, and acts accordingly, the more "virtuous" their actions are. The Golden Rule in Christianity is a recipe for accrual of good karma. It comes from actions undertaken with a higher degree of empathy.

Conversely, we can infer from a list of actions producing "bad karma" or "negative karma" that selfish acts which treat other people as objects rather than as subjects, is not virtuous. Acting with intentionality directed to objectified otherness gives you "bad karma," according to traditional sources.

Bad karma acquired is subtracted from whatever good karma you already had, leaving your net karmic balance reduced. You could end up with a negative balance like an overdrawn bank account. The exact algorithm for calculating karma is unspecified, but that's the gist of it.

Here are some "virtuous" actions that confer good karma, according to the *Tibetan Book of the Dead* and the *Yoga-Sutras*:

Generosity

Good conduct

Service to others

Rejoicing the merit of others

Hearing and offering the Dharma (the teachings)

Non-violence

Honesty

Truthfulness

Fidelity

These virtues are not all well-specified. "Good conduct," seems especially vague. Nevertheless, we notice that the list does not include actions like doing push-ups, filling the car with gas, or playing tennis. Virtuous actions are social interactions emphasizing regard for other people. It's apparently intersubjectivity that generates karma.

On the other side of the karmic ledger, some non-virtuous actions that accrue bad karma (from the same sources) include:

Killing

Stealing

Sexual misconduct

Lying

Harsh speech

Malicious gossip

Greed

Anger

The non-virtuous actions are also underspecified, but we can see they have selfishness in common, which is acting with low empathic regard for others. Is that all it takes to get to heaven, then: be nice?

Intentionality and Karma

There is an additional wrinkle to the karmic formula. You have to be self-aware of your actions, both the intentions behind them, and their consequences. If you accidentally harm someone, that's bad karma (because it's a bad consequence), but since you didn't "mean to," it's not a *lot* of bad karma. The amount of karma, good or bad, depends on how you understand each action, its intention and its expected outcome. Did you act without compassion or did you act empathically even though the outcome was not what you expected?

That contingency means non-human animals accrue no karma, according to traditional accounts. Animals are not self-aware of their motivation. Today, we might reconsider that rule based on what we know about animal intelligence.

Properly socialized adults are expected to be self-aware however, so intentionality matters. Claiming that an action that harmed someone was "unintentional," is not a defense in the metaphorical court of karma. All actions are intentional and you know what you intended regardless of how it turned out. At the very least, you should have known how it might have turned out, because the wise person considers consequences before acting.

What about children? While the process of primary socialization is underway, which can take fifteen years or more, self-awareness of one's intentionality is lower than for mature adults. With lower intentional self-awareness, the karmic consequences are decreased for children.

As soon as they are old enough to understand the consequences of their actions, children begin to accumulate consequential karma. The rule reminds me of a favorite *New Yorker* cartoon. A judge pronounces a verdict on a puppy from the high bench: "Not guilty, because puppies do such things." By the same karmic principle of intentional self-awareness, plants cannot accrue karma.

What about an evil psychopath? A psychopath lacks empathy by definition, but understands very well the consequences of their harmful actions. That person accrues bad karma like anyone else. It may not be the person's "fault," if they are constitutionally disposed to psychopathic thinking and behavior. They can't help themselves, we could argue. But the Law of Karma is not about blame. It's about intentional action and the consequences. The psychopath gets bad karma.

Another implication of the definition of karma is that it only accrues to individuals. Groups and communities do not earn karma, as they have no intentionality. Intentionality is a motivation of an individual subjectivity. Communities have the consensus of its individuals, which is metaphorical, not real self-awareness. The individual is the karmic unit.

Judgment and Value

In the context of trying to understand death as a BHN, what makes the theory of karma interesting is that karma supposedly persists across death and determines the qualities of one's "next life," assuming reincarnation. I'll take up the question of reincarnation later. For now, the relevant idea is the persistence of karma at death and how that compares to the proposed persistence of the Planck Code over any BHN.

One similarity is that neither one's Planck Code or one's accumulated karma are intersubjectively judgmental. No blame or shame is involved. The persistent values are derived from mathematic-like algorithms, objective and impersonal, based on one's intentions and actions.

Nevertheless, from examination of the rules for accruing karmic "points," it's clear that karma derives from a system of values. It's not like in basketball where you get three points for a successful shot outside the line but only two if your feet are inside the line. That's arbitrary. Positive karmic points accrue for socially-valued actions like "generosity" and negative points for acts like "cheating." An implicit theory of human morality is built into the Law of Karma.

In my reading of the history of the Law of Karma, it looks like the moral and ethical aspect came later. Originally, in the *Vedas*, the "virtuous actions" referred to proper ceremonial performances. "Good" action was correct performance of religious rites. "Bad" action was dereliction of religious duty. Later, religions such as Hinduism elaborated the concept of karmic action into the implicit moral system we know today.

Planck Karma?

The content of the Planck Code is similar in some ways to the concept of karma. The Planck code records a valenced (signed) consequence of action, but without social judgment. The values are those discussed earlier in the context of the motivational module of mind, the IMS. A positive value is returned from the IMS module to the other modules when an accommodative action satisfies the prior intentional act in part or in full. Negative values result when satisfaction is not had.

"Satisfaction" is defined in the IMS module as (a non-conceptual) assessment of change in metaphorical "distance" of SRS from its telos or ultimate goal. That ultimate goal is accommodation of all objective otherness into subjective "meness," a kind of subjective imperial triumph (details in Adams, 2021a).

The Planck Code is updated during the accommodative micro-BHN that occurs in every mental cycle. No human or divine judgment is attached to it. During "larger" BHNs, such as NREM sleep and the meditative BHN, a deeper, more systemic integration of Planck Code content may occur, making it less granular and more like a Gestalt-formation than the individual transactions. In those larger BHNs a more holistic integration of accommodative successes would presumably prevail.

We can imagine the difference between the micro-BHNs within each cycle of mental activity as somewhat "thin." The "larger" or "longer" BHNs like NREM sleep involve more integrative updates that consolidate the new material more deeply with the existing. If death is like the other BHNs then death too, would involve a process that consolidates and integrates Planck Code contents into the largest Gestalt, perhaps the "final" update of a lifetime.

The ever-developing, ever-consolidating Planck Code is the basis for rebuilding self and world after the BHN. Details on that process, called The Reconstruction, will be discussed shortly. The Planck Code is one of the three reconstructive seeds, and it seems to function similarly to the purported function of one's accumulated karma.

Planck Code is Not Karma

While the Planck Code, with its input from interactive satisfaction, is analogous in many ways to the operation of karma, the two are by no means identical. The Planck Code is not karma. The differences are important. They include:

1. The input to the evaluative algorithm for the Planck Code are degrees of intersubjective, motivational satisfaction. For karma, they are ethical actions and moral intentions.

2. Social judgment is implicit for karma but not for the Planck Code.

3. Religious implications are involved for karma but not the Planck Code.

4. Reincarnation is implicit in the idea of karma but not the Planck Code.

Calculating the Planck Code

Let's suppose for the sake of illustration that updating the Planck Code is a quasi-computational process. The IMS module, one of three implementations of the QMP architecture of mentality, is the computational engine. It has two tasks: update the Planck Code and save it against the onslaught of BHN nothingness. How could that happen?

We can look again at QMP operations. Self-relating subjectivity (SRS) comes out of a BHN emitting intentional acts. Each arc of intentionality is designed to expel the self-alien otherness that haunts the SRS. From previous analyses, we know that subjectivity's "felt otherness" is its connectedness to the field of Commodity Subjectivity.

The self-object generated by the SRS intentional act is an objectification of that feared otherness, expressed as the intersection of self and other at a moment in time. That's the essential data for the Planck Code: the quality of that interaction.

Interaction with every object is social. Not just interaction with other people and animals, but with every rock, tree and Amazon package. That's because all mental objects are SRS projections of Commodity Subjectivity, the otherness that haunts it. Some of those projected self-objects congeal into social others, easily reached by intersubjectivity. Other self-objects lack the qualities that tag them to us as intersubjective, so they appear as "brute" objects. But they're still all made of the same stuff.

If you could see your Planck Code you would marvel that such a tiny speck contained everything that defined your self and your world over your whole life. Try as you might, you couldn't read it. Like DNA, the Planck Code is not a blueprint for anything. It has to be observed behaving to understand what it is and what it does.

Conclusion

I've described some ways in which the Planck Code is comparable (but not identical) to the concept of Karma. The useful points of comparison are:

1. Both survive the oblivion of a Black Hole of Nothingness, which is death in the case of karma, any BHN for the Planck Code.

2. Both contain information about the quality of experience up to the start of the BHN.

3. Neither is intersubjectively judgmental but algorithmic in nature, derived from the qualities of lived experience.

4. Both are instrumental in reconstructing self and world after the BHN terminates.

Now we enough conceptual grounding to consider further the BHN of interest in this essay, the BHN of death.

The Start of Death

The working hypothesis is that death is a BHN like the others. That's despite the fact that, unlike other BHNs, we have never died and have no "experience" of death. However, all BHNs are non-experiences by definition anyway, and can only be studied "from the outside."

Looking at death as a kind of BHN, we would say it has a beginning, an end, and some interior dynamics. We can also say that certain "seeds" of experience survive it to "germinate" after its end.

Let's take a closer look at these "regions" of death:

1. The start of death
2. The workings of death
3. The end of death

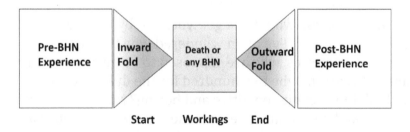

Figure 3. Context of a BHN

The Start

The Inward Fold of death is when we begin dying, around age 35. That's the age at which most people are past the growth period that plateaus in the late 20's. After 35 or so, with variation among individuals, it's "all downhill." The body inexorably begins to lose capacity, ending in death. That makes sense from an evolutionary point of view where the purpose of life is reproduction. If you're not reproducing anymore you're just using up good resources that youngsters need. You might as well begin decomposing.

We don't take a strictly biological view of life of course, especially not in this essay which emphasizes the first-person, experiential point of view. In terms of experience, the second half of life is the best part. That's when you finally have your head screwed on straight and you're free of parental, educational, hormonal and other tyrannies and can pursue your life's work, love, and interests. Nevertheless, biological death governs what you can do.

No matter what you are engaged in mentally, you *will* run out of time. Death is not optional. Why should that be? It is not difficult to imagine a world in which a person chooses death when they are "ready." Time of death could be like when you are enjoying dinner at a restaurant with friends and you realize it's time to give up your table. Or like a wonderful day at the beach when you think, "The sun is going down now. It's time to go." Why isn't that how death works?

Or maybe you would just get worn out by living and decide you've had enough. I've often wondered why that doesn't happen to vampires, who are supposed to be immortal. After a hundred years, maybe two hundred for the dull-witted ones, wouldn't life become repetitive and boring? New gizmos and thrills would be invented, new plagues and wars would erupt, but eventually, life would be same-old, and any reasonable vampire would decide they've had enough.

For us, the Grim Reaper knocks when your number's up regardless of whether you're "ready." That's how all the BHNs work. You might be able to defer a BHN like sleep a little bit, but it *will* get you at some point.

Why Death is Involuntary

The onset of death might be similar to the BHN of sleep. Perhaps it can be slightly deferred, as sleep can be. More people die shortly after their birthday than immediately before it. The distribution of deaths should be statistically random, but it isn't. That implies an ability to slightly manage death's onset.

Looking at the social context of death and other BHNs, we can find good reasons why it is not optional.

1. Embodiment.

Minds are embodied, and bodies die. We cannot specify the exact nature of embodiment, but we know that minds only occur in bodies. Even when we attempt to discern the interior of a BHN using the Marco Polo Method (Adams, 2023a) we come to "The Uncrossable Plain," a vast, featureless terrain one knows intuitively not to venture into. That probably is a deep mental representation of the unknowable details of one's biology.

We lack much introspective access into our embodiment, and that's too bad. If we had it, introspective self-diagnosis of illness, disease, and even genetic disorders would be possible. We must settle for whatever knowledge we can glean from sensorimotor consciousness (the SMC module of mind), such as pains and rashes, exploratory performance, and similar indirect sources. To date, those don't offer us much clue about why death is involuntary.

From other BHNs, we see that crossing the metaphorical event horizon into the BHN is also involuntary, despite good preparation. We prepare for sleep, and we even see it coming. The Inward Fold is the period approaching a BHN when consciousness fades out. During that transition, some observation can be done. We can note loss of clear thinking, increase in dissociative thoughts, feelings, and images, slowing body rhythms, and loss of bodily and world-awareness. These are all gradual steps on the Inward Fold to entering a BHN.

But the exact moment of "falling asleep" is still involuntary. You don't get to decide when to cross that line. Nor does it seem to be a steady and predictable diminution of mental and bodily activity like a car driving into the distance until it disappears. Rather, at some arbitrary and seemingly abrupt moment of hypnagogic wooziness, one is simply "gone." The same is true for the onset of anesthesia and the meditative BHN.

The Inward Fold of the meditative BHN can be meticulous and lengthy, especially when learning how to navigate it. Even after learning that process, one can self-observe closely during the Inward Fold to see when one is nearing the precipice, but the moment of mental oblivion is still not a choice. It just happens.

We could attribute the experiential uncertainty of the onset of the BHN to biological processes we are mentally unable to discern. We can control the body, even the behavior of the brain to some extent, but only up to a point. After that point, it's "out of our hands." It's likely therefore, that a person could see immanent death approaching, just as we can make out the edge of most BHNs as we approach them. But the moment of "crossing" would always be involuntary.

Why should it be like that? Why *don't* we have introspective access to all aspects of embodiment? An easy answer is to remember the Uroboros, the mythical snake that swallows its tail. It's a paradox because it presents a morphological limit to the process of self-dissolution. The same is true for any closed (well-defined) system of knowledge, as mathematician Goedel proved with his famous "incompleteness theorems" (Goedel, 1931, translated by Van Heijenoort, 1967). No system can fully account for itself. Apparently, that includes the SLM mental system. However, that principle just affirms the paradox without explaining it.

A better answer is that a fundamental alienation from embodiment is necessary for individual mentality to exist at all. We must absolutely believe in our embodiment because biological uniqueness guarantees psychological uniqueness. Without a body, we would psychologically be "nowhere." We cannot afford to be casual about giving up embodiment. It is too important to be trusted to error-prone cognitive choice. The final onset of any BHN, including death, is unpredictable because our mental constitution wisely prevents us from fully understanding our embodiment. If we understood it, you know we'd tinker with it.

2. License to Live.

In Adams (2021b), I proposed that we each have a metaphorical License to Live. It's an implicit contract with society. When the contract expires, you must die.

The license is a set of tacit, barely-conscious expectations, trans-personal and sub-conceptual. It says you can live about a hundred years, not much more. If a person claims to be five-hundred years old, we are skeptical. Everyone knows that's not in the license.

As medicine and health improve over the centuries, social expectations change and so does the license. The median life expectancy was, only a few decades ago, sixty-five for males. Someone living to be a hundred was extremely rare. It isn't anymore, so the community has tacitly updated its expectations and its implicit license.

Under this idea, you die when you're expected to because there's nothing else to do. When your time's up, you are still cared for, but you have absorbed about as much socialization from the community as your capacity allows and as the community is willing to give. When that happens, you give up your license and are re-absorbed into the community's consciousness as a memory.

What if you don't want to go? You can hang around for a while, but you'll become socially isolated. You'll outlive most of your friends and family, lose your connections, certainly your health, eventually your wealth. Your children and grandchildren will care for you but you will sense their indulgence.

Different societies have different regard for old people, but in fact oldsters require more time and more social, physical, and economic, resources than youngsters. You can live in an institutional setting with other old people as long as you don't run out of money, but it will eventually become clear that you are superfluous to society. With increasing social isolation, it seems more reasonable to call it quits. You expect to die, and so does everybody else, so you do.

That's a socially-oriented restatement of the fact that death is involuntary. The advantage of that approach is that it does not directly invoke biological explanation. We shouldn't use biology to account for the end of experience when biology does not explain experience. The License to Live approach offers an alternative.

3. The Transindividual.

Philosopher Gilbert Simondon (cited by Combes, 2013) suggests that death is actually a step up, not an unmitigated loss. While it's true that you lose your body, your personality, identity, and all distinctive qualities when you die, that is offset by merging into the "transindividual," a non-personal, relational community.

While you're alive, he says, you are inherently full of tensions that arise from relations between you and your community. No amount of psychotherapy can relieve those tensions because they are intrinsic to the nature of individuality. This idea is not so different from my definition of self-relating subjectivity as a dynamic tension between ipseity and otherness.

Upon death of the individual, per Simondon's ideas, internal tensions are resolved when the dynamic of individuality transduces into a new kind of relation, the transindividual. The transindividual is a "higher-order" relation with others.

Mapping Simondon's ontology to my phenomenology, I could say that the prospect of transindividual relations seems attractive to the individual, even a lure, a reason to die. The opportunity to become part of the transindividual motivates dying to be more than just a single individual.

We experience a transindividual moment when a person says things like "Yay, we won the big game!" The speaker personally didn't win it, nor did the listener. But the intersubjective "we" momentarily transforms both of them into a larger collective identity that includes the team of athletes and their spectators. It feels good to be part of that. It's celebratory.

When you die, you might become permanently part of a transindividual community like that. That seems attractive to an individual. That's the basis of Simondon's estimation that the transindividual is a "step up."

I describe the situation differently. While it is fair to say, as Simondon does, that at death, de-individuation occurs, it's not a good thing.

A subjectivity's motivation is *not* to join or merge with otherness. To do that would be oblivion, a total loss of self in the other. That prospect is exactly why most people fear death. Nobody wants oblivion. To do so is a perverse "death wish."

Instead, individual subjectivity (SRS) seeks omnipotence and omniscience, which it would seemingly achieve if it could absorb all otherness into itself. It would not perish, but on the contrary, *be all that is*. It's misleading to suggest that the individual is attracted to de-individuation even for the lure of transindividualism. No normal SRS desires de-individuation for any reason.

Perhaps it's not fair to compare Simondon's ontology to my first-person approach to metaphysics. His comments concerning motivation are indirect and the ideas only implied. He's not trying to do a first-person analysis. Still, any philosophy that suggests that the threat of personal oblivion is overshadowed by the promise of transindividual relations is unconvincing. Loss of self is oblivion. Most people fear permanent oblivion.

Transindividual relations might seem attractive if one supposes it means continued individualism in a transindividual state, which is a contradiction. I think Simondon makes that mistake.

4. Boredom.

A simplistic explanation for the involuntary onset of death is boredom. In pursuit of its telos, SRS continuously nibbles away at the objective otherness that taunts it. It does that by accommodating whole and partial objects to itself. That process takes place over a lifetime. It is in fact the process of experiencing life.

We can imagine that at some phase of maturity, perhaps in old age, the SRS has consumed the majority of not-self otherness of which it is aware. The world and other people all more-or-less make sense. One has a fairly good understanding of oneself. Few mysteries remain. It seems like everything's been done and nothing is really new.

Whether true or not, if that is the state of the SRS motivation, it has basically run out of things to do. It is bloated with experience, knowledge, and self-understanding. Life has become repetitive and less interesting.

In such a state of "otherness-fatigue," intentional activity becomes less intense and new self-objects become minor variations on well-practiced themes. In such a situation, the SRS might essentially give up and cease operation. The result would be collapse of the QMP cycle of experience, which is tantamount to death.

Hospice workers have reported that many patients seem to just give up and die of "exhaustion." It's difficult to interpret these reports because palliative drugs are often involved in end-of-life treatment. But at least "boredom" or "exhaustion" with life seems like a plausible explanation for the onset of death. It wouldn't be so different from falling asleep.

I suggest that the individual motivation in such cases is to find peace and quiet, relief from the noise and stress of embodied living. The person seeks the telos which is disembodied wholeness and stillness. If a person has some "phantasmagorical" ideas about death, such as cosmic unity or heavenly bliss, the strategy of giving up on life might seem attractive.

The "boredom" account of death's onset, while plausible, falls short. It still does not explain why the moment of death is involuntary.

5. Self-preservation

Paradoxically, the onset of death may be involuntary simply because we "don't want anything to do with it." Typically, the mind ceases before the body does. In cases of violence and accident, the whole person is wiped out in the same instant, but there are no documented cases where the body perishes but the mind persists for a while. Perhaps out-of-body near-death experiences are like that, but in fact the body did *not* perish because the person lived.

Has anyone ever correctly had the thought, "I am dead now?" That person would be having mental experience after the cessation of the body. That's not possible, because minds only occur in bodies. Could there be borderline conditions? I don't know but doubt it.

Most commonly, a dying person gradually loses their mental faculties before the moment of biological death. That loss can occur over years in the case of dementia. It happens that way because we don't want to say goodbye. The dying person knows they are "leaving." They're either at the station or have already boarded the train to nowhere. The mental pain of impending loss and forthcoming oblivion is too great to bear so mental agency gives up in advance in self-protection. Maybe that's why the moment of death is involuntary.

Inhibiting Force

Considering the foregoing discussion, no clear explanation emerges for why death is involuntary. The possibilities mentioned merely reaffirm that it is, or deny that it isn't.

For the meditative BHN or for falling asleep, the "last" mental cycle during the Inward Fold is the one terminated by nothingness (judged in retrospect, upon recovery). You never know which intentional act is going to be the last.

In the Inward Fold of the meditative BHN, we see it coming when we systematically inhibit sensory input, proprioception, mental chatter, and motivational impulses. If you do it right, at some unpredictable moment of focus, everything disappears and you "enter" the BHN. The same process holds, in a less disciplined and predictable way when we "fall" asleep. Morpheus, the god of sleep, decides when to take you.

But what is the force that allows us to "shut down" wakeful activity in mind and body to get ready for Morpheus? It is not called motivation, because motivation is one of the things you must shut down to enter a meditative BHN. Agitated motivation can prevent you from falling asleep, as when you're intensely worried about something. You need to let go of the worry. But how do you do that? How can worry let go of itself?

Preparing for sleep and approaching the meditative BHN is a motivated process, but a self-inhibitory kind of motivation. You're motivated to *not* do anything. Sometimes we call that self-control or self-discipline.

Is self-control a kind of motivation? Yes and no. Often, self-control fights against other motivation. Sometimes self-control wins, sometimes it doesn't. That's the dynamic of mental conflict. So it is useful to conceptualize the Inhibiting Force of self-control separately from the rest of the Motivating Force.

Morpheus does not hang upside-down in a cave during the day. He (or she or they) bursts into action when the Inhibiting Force overcomes the Motivating Force, inviting a BHN. That's as close to a voluntary BHN as we can get.

Conclusion

We've established that the exact onset of death is necessarily involuntary. We did that by examining other known BHNs closely. We have as a working assumption that death is a BHN like all the others.

Some BHNs are highly approachable. Going right up to the doorstep of the meditative BHN is about as voluntary as one can get. Other approaches are semi-voluntary, such as falling asleep or submitting to anesthesia. Still others offer hardly any voluntary control, such as dying. Some are entirely involuntary, such as the micro-BHNs of the QMP mental cycle.

That's a wide range of voluntary control as we approach a BHN. But the final plunge is always involuntary. But once you're "in," then what happens?

Let's turn to what goes on "inside" the BHN. We can't know directly, but we can make inferences.

The Workings of Death

We want to know what goes on inside a BHN, and that includes the BHN of death. This is not about "the process of dying." That was discussed in the previous chapter and is a well-researched medical topic. We're interested in what happens *after* the moment of death.

We can't introspect our way into a BHN, but we can observe it from the outside. For example, we know that after a person dies, the body decomposes. But in this essay, we're most interested in the psychological journey, not the body. What happens to the "interior person" at death?

A simple-minded answer is "nothing." When you're dead, you're just gone. Dead means oblivion and that means nothing remains of the interior (mental) person.

But that's not a complete story. For example, we know that a recently deceased person continues on for a while as a memory in collective minds of the community. An obvious example is the funeral service. Is the deceased person "present" at the funeral service? Mostly no, not in a first-person way.

There is no "first-person" experience remaining of the deceased that could possibly be at the funeral. That's the 'N' in BHN. Yet there is collective experience that defines the intersubjective context that the deceased occupied. The Funeral-goers actively engage memory of the deceased.

Since individuals are always defined by their community, the community's memory of each person is a kind of non-personal perseverance of the individual. That's from a third-person, or "public" point of view. The deceased person knew before dying that this would be the case.

It is wrong to say that when a person's body dies, absolutely nothing is left. A person is also a node in a social network. What happens to the network when one node goes dark? Activity flows around it. The dark node is noticed and its absence is accommodated. The psychological ("mental") person is therefore not entirely lost, at least not right away, even when all first-person activity has ceased.

Nothing personal survives a BHN. The "person" is gone, gone, gone. But is there *anything* left inside a BHN? From analysis of other BHNs, we can say yes.

Commodity Subjectivity

Inside a BHN there is still subjectivity. It's not the kind of subjectivity we know from introspection. Commodity Subjectivity is entirely impersonal, non-individual, and unknowing. It was described earlier as one of the seeds of mentality that survive any BHN.

Simondon (cited by Combes, 2013) describes a condition similar to Commodity Subjectivity as the "preindividual field." It's pre-individual because it is not any one person's state of being. It is the communal state of being prior to individuation.

By contrast, an individual SRS has a "membrane" or boundary around it like one raindrop does. That defines its location in time and space. Commodity Subjectivity doesn't have that. It is more like pond water. It contains no individual drops. Commodity Subjectivity in a BHN is a field, not a node.

Besides being bounded, individuated SRS is (proto-) self-aware of its existence and simultaneously of that-which-is not-itself, the "otherness" that haunts its existence. Those two aspects of SRS, self-awareness and other-awareness do not get along. Their internal tension is what makes SRS forever dynamic.

Clinician and phenomenologist Zahavi (2006), described SRS as "bifurcated" into self and otherness. Simonden (cited by Grosz, 2017) said the individual was "disparated" into a productive tension between closely related but incompatible orders. Borrowing from thermodynamics, he called the tension between domains a "metastable" state.

Commodity subjectivity is not divided. It is therefore not self-relating. In some sense, Commodity Subjectivity is "pure" subjectivity because it contains no trace of objectivity or otherness. For that very reason, however, it is also incapable of participating in mentality.

Action Inside a BHN

What does Commodity Subjectivity *do* inside a BHN? BHNs are active despite being opaque. For example, they transform objectivity to subjectivity and the reverse.

At the whole-person level of analysis, we observe that the meditative BHN is psychologically active because after it, we see marked increases in synchronicity and intuition in the Outward Fold and subsequent experience. The correlation of that with the BHN suggests that those changes are due to something that happens during the BHN.

In the morning after several hours of sleep, we often wake up with "fresh ideas" or a "new outlook" and the like. When we have a difficult decision to make, we often are advised to "sleep on it." Such indications suggest that the BHN of sleep is psychologically active.

From the functions of the micro-BHNs of the QMP mental cycle, we deduce that they are active on the inside. From other ordinary BHNs, we deduce the same. Let's see if we can zoom in on that activity.

A BHN Story

We've already decided that the micro-BHNs of the QMP cycle are not empty. They must, for logical and systemic reasons, "contain" at least:

1. Commodity Subjectivity
2. The Motivating Force
3. The Planck Code

How do these entities and influences interact? I suggest a scenario based on MPM analysis, a kind of storytelling based on intuition stimulated by multiple sources. One of the sources for this story is intuition in the Outward Folds of meditative BHNs. Another is high-level imagery from quantum physics (e.g., Ball, 2018; Herbert, 1985) and chaos theory (Campuzano, 2018). The third source is the post-humanist philosopher Simondon's notion of the preindividual (Simondon, 2020).

A blend of such ideas becomes a story, a speculation about what might happen inside the BHN. That speculation can be taken seriously because of the principle of disjunct causality that underlies the MPM methodology (Adams, 2023a). That's how to look inside a BHN. Doing that, what do we see?

We imagine un-individuated Commodity Subjectivity (CS) as a surface representing a field of energy. I imagine it to have a lattice-work of orthogonal reference lines. The CS field is not calm. On the contrary, it is a high-tension field of energy.

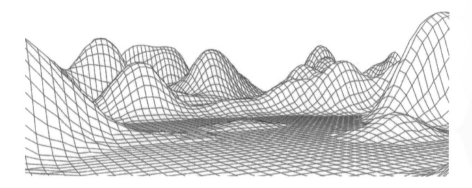

Figure 4. Image of the Interior of a BHN

The energy is the Motivating Force, a psychological energy. It's not mental motivation that anybody could feel, nor physical energy like electromagnetism. The term "energy" is re-fitted with non-physical, psychological meaning. The CS field is throbbing with Motivating Force and has no way of releasing it—no way because CS is not personal, so there's no point of view that could release energy into mental and behavioral expression.

The CS abides in its dynamic state until something happens that precipitates a change. That event is an update of a Planck Code. It happens at the moment of transition between ordinary mentality and its dissolution into the BHN.

The update of the Planck Code is a disturbance in the CS field. That disturbance precipitates the emergence of a new individual from the plane of the field. An analogy is what happens with a supersaturated liquid. When a seed is introduced, crystals immediately begin to grow around the seed. The Planck Code would be that seed.

The change in the Planck Code provokes the field to form a node, represented in *Figure 4* by one of the hills or mountains. The node is bounded, and that defines an individual. That's the process of individuation. The new individual remains attached to the field but can be counted as a separate "thing."

In this imagery, individuals are never fully separate from the field. What seems to us like autonomous billiard-ball persons banging about the world actually have their psychological roots firmly planted in the mud of non-individual Commodity Subjectivity. As individuals, we are biologically free-standing, but this account is about psychology. As psyches, our "mental feet" are always attached to the communal field. Each individual is a mere bulbous eruption of the field.

In the MPM vision of the CS field, bubbles of subjectivity arise at various times and locations as they do in gently boiling water. The diagram of *Figure 4* should properly be a video showing the various hills and mountains rising and falling at different rates.

Communities, defined by regions of the field are where Planck Codes aggregate by spontaneous self-organization due to their content similarities. Each "hill" of individuality rises above the surface of CS, forming a local zone of energy and morphology that constitutes a mini-entropy-reduction for the rest of the field.

The individual, by rising above the surface of the field, creates an area partially separated from the ground. The separation is spatial in this representation. We tacitly assume that the separation takes place in time so the essential features of an individual are that it has a unique "location" in space and time. That's what defines "an individual."

Of course, in the BHN there is neither space nor time, but the MPM method produces stories, and they must use the language of ordinary experience. This is a story of individuation. The story can inform one's understanding of the interiority of a BHN. Stories are not meant to be taken literally, only suggestively.

Conclusion

Death is a kind of BHN, so the foregoing describes what goes on there, too. Further, like all BHNs, death must terminate at some point. Let's next take a closer look at how a BHN ends.

The End of Death

When you go to bed at night, how do you know you'll ever wake up again? Maybe we should fear sleep.

The scientific account of waking up is that the brain ramps up production of chemicals like dopamine in response to signals from the "biological clock," the suprachiasmic nucleus of the hypothalamus. Other chemical and neurological processes also operate on a diurnal rhythm with the result that we reliably awaken. In a coma, that process fails due to brain pathology and you don't wake up. In death, there is *no* brain activity, so you never wake up. So, is biology the answer?

It can't be. A BHN is not a biological condition. A BHN is a gap in mentality, a loss of self-awareness, an experiential nothingness. There is no such thing as a BHN in the biological domain, which is about bodies, not minds. So we need to continue searching for some other explanation for why BHNs terminate.

Why a BHN Terminates

This is a deceptively simple problem. Deceptive because it presupposes the point of view of an ordinary, conscious person who, in retrospect, says, "I just had a gap in my experience." It might have been sleep, a meditative BHN, an alcoholic blackout, a spell under anesthesia, or any of a number of familiar BHNs. But the BHN must already be over in order to notice it. To ask why a BHN terminates means it already happened. Like Minerva, we only know it after it's done.

What if we take a "Marco Polo" point of view, the imaginary outlook of a traveler into the interior of a BHN? Marco Polo is someone who leaves the Walled Garden of ordinary experience and journeys into the inside of a Black Hole of Nothingness. As a fictitious entity, the Marco Polo traveler can maintain a point of view.

When we do that exercise, we see (imagine) that what begins the termination of a BHN is the process of individuation. Individuation is when a new individual arises from the surface of Commodity Subjectivity. The individual swells up from the surface like a bubble or a hill. That bubble becomes "an individual" with respect to the field. It's not a *person*. It's not even a completely separate entity. It's just an identifiable, countable region of subjectivity, an *individual* region in the undifferentiated field.

That individual is made of Commodity Subjectivity, the stuff of the field from which it arises. But as an individual, its subjectivity acquires qualities that the field lacks. The new qualities include unique location in (metaphorical) space and time because the individual has become a countable entity. But there's more than that.

The new individual is energized by the Motivating Force (MF). That force is now bounded by the membrane that defines the individual. Bound, contained, subjectivity has a different quality than unbounded, unconstrained Commodity Subjectivity.

We can imagine that the MF in the bounded region is under more "pressure" like a gas compressed into a container, or that it has higher electrical potential, like electrons segregated in a capacitor. This is psychological energy, not physical, so the parameters are not literally those.

Imagine though, that bounded MF gives individual subjectivity a higher "voltage" than the unbounded MF. Since the individual remains attached to the CS plane at bottom, there is a charge gradient across the individual. It's high near the top where the individual is crisply bounded, and almost zero at the bottom where the individual is connected to the field.

The higher and lower energy zones of subjectivity are affected by the Planck Code. Flowing "upward" through the Planck Code, the MF of individual subjectivity arises.

Figure 5. Individuation from the CS Grid

Individual subjectivity is no longer purely the commodity type, but the self-relating type. Subjectivity within the individual has become polarized, which psychologically, means (proto-) self-aware of a range of motivating energies within itself. MF modified by the Planck Code creates tension between high-voltage MF of the bounded part of the individual, and the low-voltage part that's rooted to the field.

We (fully-formed, tripartite minds) experience the high voltage part as the Cartesian sense of "I-am-ness." The less distinct, lower-energy MF at the bottom, near the commodity surface, is felt as a shadow, a not-me "otherness." Individual subjectivity thus has the internal tension of self-relatedness. It is a SRS, no longer purely CS.

The individual subjectivity attempts to equilibrate between high and low-energy regions of its MF. A "discharge" of MF voltage from the individual to the CS is an attempt at that. We would experience that change in the mature mind as an intentional act directed to an object of otherness.

The new SRS's first official act is to issue an arc of MF energy (intentionality) away from itself in an attempt to expel the otherness at its base. It's as if the newly individuated node looks down at its feet, sees them stuck in the mud of Commodity Subjectivity, and says "What the hell?"

Individual SRS sees itself mired in a "foreign" not-self otherness that should be expelled. It does not appreciate its intrinsic connection to the ground of all subjectivity. It tries to shake off the mud with an intentional outburst.

The first intentional arc of SRS is thus a self-expression, a blend of motivational energy comprised of bounded self-relatedness and rejection of unbounded not-self otherness. The intentional discharge becomes a hybrid self-object which hardens into a fully alien, free-standing object with respect to SRS. The first half of the first mental cycle has been accomplished (see Figure 1).

In the next instant, the free-standing object just created is partially reabsorbed into the SRS in an act of accommodation (again see Figure 1). With that, the Marco Polo traveler can say that one complete mental cycle has occurred and that is what defines a QMP cycle. At that moment mentality and experience are defined and the BHN has ended.

But Who is it?

The newly-formed, post-BHN individual has executed the barest of QMP mental cycles. This minimal "mind" has no world other than its own self-object, no context, no self-identity, and no memory because it has no other experience. It is a brand-new entity, virtually a blank slate.

Our fictitious Marco Polo traveler returns to the Walled Garden of experience when the BHN is over. We know that nothing personal survives a BHN. Yet after it's over, the world in the Garden is familiar, and ordinary experience seems to pick up where it left off. If the post-BHN individual is a blank slate, we need to account for the rich and familiar experience post-BHN.

Continuity of Mind and World

Two possibilities could explain the similarity of experience before and after a BHN:

A. The individual coming out of a BHN recalls what self and world were like before and interprets subsequent experience according to that mnemonic.

B. The post-BHN self and world are completely new, but the new world includes "dinosaur bones" that imply a long history. The person accepts the new world and its history without suspecting it was all just freshly minted.

Possibility A:

Recall of the pre-BHN world requires that memory of the former world survives the BHN. But that is contrary to what we know about BHNs. Embodiment does not survive a BHN (that's from the first-person point of view). The mind disappears by definition. What could "memory" even mean without a mind?

Another problem is the recall. What entity would recall how things were pre-BHN? The idea of self-recalling memory doesn't make sense. Recall presupposes a mentality that can do it. But the just-emerged mentality of one QMP cycle hardly has the resources to recall anything from anywhere.

Then too, after emergence from a BHN, the world doesn't really feel like a memory. It seems like the actual world. It does not appear in a "mnemonic mode of presentation," as Husserl would say. For at least these three reasons, the hypothesis that the post-BHN world is a recalled memory of the pre-BHN world is not plausible. That leaves the second possibility.

Possibility B:

What about a brand-new world after the BHN? After you come out, self and world are rebuilt from the (metaphorical) ground up. Is that plausible? It might not seem so at first, but let's take a closer look.

Scope of the New World

The new world does not have to be built in every detail from quarks to cosmos. That's not how you experience the world. That's an objective, omniscient view that nobody has. The actual world you live in is much smaller. You only know your own experience as defined by your history, geography, and culture.

The reconstructed post-BHN world only needs to encompass your personal experience of it, not the entire objective world.

Even for a personal world, the amount of detail from a lifetime of experience might first seem unmanageably large. But it isn't.

Every person constructed their entire first-person world in every detail, starting from virtually nothing. It took a lifetime to do it, but you did it, I did it, everybody and every animal does it. The entire first-person world *can* be built from scratch. We know that because that's how each person's experiential world came to be.

Could it be done *again* in a few microseconds upon exiting a BHN? Imagine your entire self and world, starting from essentially nothing, expanding to everything, *foop!* in an instant. Is that plausible?

Elastic Time

There is no time in a BHN. Outside a BHN, proper time in ordinary life is defined by experience of embodied change. What's between those endpoints of no time and experienced time?

In the elastic period of transition between the nothingness of the BHN and the "everything" of the wakeful world time stretches from zero to a hundred percent of normal experience.

If we assume reconstitution of self and world takes place close to the horizon of the BHN in the Outward Fold, time would be very compressed and the creation could happen in an instant. An analogy is to what cosmologists call the "great inflation" of the universe shortly after the Big Bang.

The reconstruction of the world would happen exactly as construction of it did the first time around when you were growing up. The *process* of world-construction is exactly the same, a lifetime of socialization and learning. It's a well-documented process. It could occur again near the horizon of the BHN. It would just be on a shorter time scale.

Is that plausible? Consider that the 2023 Nobel Prize in physics was awarded for research on the attosecond scale. An attosecond is a quintillionth of a second. There are more attoseconds in a second than there have been seconds since the Big Bang. That short of a time period is virtually inconceivable to us. Could any meaningful event occur in such a short time scale?

The Nobel-laureates measured the change of an electron's position within its atomic orbital on the attosecond scale. Big, important things do happen in very short time frames. The idea that a person's entire experienced world could be constructed "from scratch" after emergence from a BHN is completely plausible.

The result of that near-instantaneous construction is a full and complete world with you in it. It's a brand new world, objectively speaking. But from your first-person perspective, it is just the familiar world and life you have always known "since the beginning." Only the Marco Polo traveler has the point of view that makes a different interpretation possible.

Social Relations

One might object that in the "original," or conventional case of world-construction on the time scale of decades, the process of world-building involved continuous interaction with the social community. The experience of teaching and learning, trial and error, conjecture and refutation—all that is socialization, and that's how each of us built the "original" first-person world, in collaboration with others, over a lifetime.

In a post-BHN instantaneous world-construction, where is that social community? It's there. Other people exist (for you) as you know them. They don't exist separately from the world-building process. They expand with your world just as they did in the original construction, from "Mother" (or other primary caregiver, N=1) to other family members, friends, teachers, collaborators, and finally the whole social world of people you eventually came to know. As the community expands, so does the world.

Personal world-building is concordant with expansion of social interactions. There are some subtle differences, because other people are both subjects and objects for us. I'll dig into the details of that later. But in short, every individuated person is always connected to Commodity Subjectivity, so it's not a stretch to imagine being connected to other individual subjectivities from the beginning.

Feeling of Continuity

The post-BHN world may be re-created in an instant after every BHN, yet when it's done, it doesn't seem like a new world. The people we know are the ones we've known since childhood. One's motives and goals are remembered from before. Our clothing still fits because we remember where and when we acquired it for a familiar body.

It's as if the BHN didn't really happen and the world is the world it's always been. And for most BHNs, that is the experience. BHNs are not noticed at all. It's only when a BHN is noticed that we remark on it. We then remind ourselves that our experience and knowledge of history is continuous. The BHN was just a blip. That's the only case that demands explanation.

What World is This?

The new, inflation-driven, post-BHN world could not be "my" world because all of "me" was erased upon entry into the BHN. So whose world is it?

Trick question! There *is no* pre-BHN world from that point of view. It was totally erased. It was obliterated upon entry into the BHN. There is nothing to remember. You have only the point of view that you have now, and *the* world is *your* world, the only one you have ever known. All your memories of the world you live in now are real. Everything you think happened, happened, just very quickly.

Only Marco Polo could "objectively" compare the pre- and post-BHN worlds. You and I, ordinary mortals, have no point of view except the actual ones we have. Marco Polo says our world is newly-constructed, but he must be nuts.

A gap in autobiographical memory is recalled when a BHN was noticed. If you had an anesthetic "blackout," you are missing some presumed experience from when you were "out." The doctors tell you an hour went by and now you have a surgical wound and groggy consciousness. You remember lying on the table and waiting for the anesthetic to "kick in," and then you remember waking up in a recovery room. In between is nothing. So you accept the public story of an operating room with anesthetic. That patches over the gap: you were "under."

The gap in experience is thus conceptualized and objectified as an ordinary event. We don't take an ordinary BHN as something that presents deep metaphysical questions. The continuity of ordinary experience has priority. Everything must fit into the autobiographical narrative, including BHNs. So they become conceptualized as blips, gaps, or BHNs.

However, a fictional Marco Polo traveler with a pseudo-omniscient point of view might say, "Not so fast. You were in a BHN and everything about you was erased. Now you live in a brand-new, post-BHN, reconstructed world. Joke's on you."

But that's not the reality of life in the Garden. Here, the present remains securely attached to the past, with BHN anomalies conceptualized as exceptions, narratively patched up and painted over.

A New View of Death

The basis of the MPM as an epistemological method (Adams, 2023a) is the idea that even fictional stories come from somewhere. Arbitrary stories are not possible. Even the wildest, most remote human associations are grounded in some kind of personal experience. That's true even for crazy dream stories. Freud knew this.

The MPM is not about psychoanalyzing the imagination. It's not even deconstruction. Rather, one looks at themes of the "travel journal" with the assumption that they reflect patterns of sub-cognitive or transpersonal bits of knowledge not readily conceptualized. In that way we hope to discern areas of reality not open to direct examination, areas like the non-experience of a BHN.

The River of Forgetfulness

In my speculative novel, *Polters* (Adams, 2023b) characters traveled into the land of the dead but retained their ordinary sense of self and their point of view. To get there, they had to cross a great river. Why a river? Because intuitively, it feels like that's what happens when moving from ordinary thinking into the fictional world of imagination, from the ordinary point of view into the Marco Polo point of view.

In ancient Greek mythology, the River Lethe (rhymes with leafy), named after the God of Oblivion, was one of the five rivers of the underworld. The river's waters induced complete forgetfulness of life before entering the land of the dead.

In Plato's *Myth of Er,* travelers in the land of the dead had to drink from the River Lethe before they could enter heaven. Such a river appears in many fictional contexts, from Virgil and Dante to Purcell's *Dido and Aeneas.* I call it the River of Forgetfulness to distance the idea from identification with Hades, heaven, and other mythologies, from the Greeks and Romans onward. I want it to be just a metaphorical river that separates two realities.

In a "Marco Polo" description of Otherland (Adams, 2023a), The River of Forgetfulness interrupts the only road in and out of the Walled Garden of Life. You must wade across the river on the way out, which makes you forget about ever having lived in the Garden. On the return journey, you have to cross the river again, and upon re-entering the Garden, you remember virtually nothing about Otherland. It's kind of like going under an anesthetic. The two domains are almost completely unconnected.

Why does this powerful river-image of amnesia appear so strongly in multiple mythological tales? It emphasizes how important it is to forget everything about living before entering the land of the dead. But why? And on the other side, why does one emerge from a BHN with no memory of what went on in there?

The River describes an empirical fact: one does pass into oblivion when entering a Black Hole of Nothingness such as dreamless sleep, the meditative BHN, and the micro-BHNs. People have known that fact since there were self-aware people. That's why we say "I was knocked out," or "I blacked out." It's an explanation for amnesia. The "out" refers to the nothingness unremembered. Oblivion and its amnesia are captured and objectified in the idea of a river as the boundary between experience and nothingness.

Real rivers separate different terrains, and often different cultures and nations. A river is a good image for separating mental domains, too. The River of Forgetfulness also separates subjectivity from objectivity.

If subjectivity and objectivity were not kept separate, they would immediately combine. Each act of intentionality would be instantly satisfied by complete accommodation. Every projected object would be immediately consumed. Like an electrical short-circuit, mentality would be over the moment it started. Subjectivity and objectivity must be insulated to maintain the polarity and the sequences of the mental cycle. The River does that.

Forgetting and Erasing

To forget is also to *know* you have forgotten. If you forget something and don't know you forgot it (and are never reminded), that's the same as if the thing never was. That's not forgetting, that's erasure. Forgetting retains a link to the forgotten experience. Erasure is obliteration without that link. The river could have been named the River of Erasure, but that's less catchy.

After crossing the River of Forgetfulness into a BHN, you suffer erasure. There's nothing left to remember and no chance of recalling what has been erased after entry into a BHN. Erasure is what separates experience from the BHN and the BHN from experience.

Fortunately, the oblivion wrought by the river is not 100% throughout the mind. There are hints of unconceptualized experience that can be recovered in a non-cognitive way after crossing the river. That's what makes the Marco Polo Method possible. It's not remembering of what was forgotten but an intuitive reconstruction of what was erased.

Tiny bits of experience survive the BHN crossing. We have identified three of those bits: Commodity Subjectivity, the Motivating Force, and the Planck Code.

Both Sides

From the pseudo-omniscient point of view that the MPM provides, we can imagine what it would be like to abide inside the BHN. From the outside, a BHN looks like a hard black marble of nothing.

But when you're (imaginatively) inside a BHN, it's not nothing. It's just a different terrain than what you're used to. I described such an imaginary terrain in Adams (2023a). Inside the BHN we would expect to see a field of Commodity Subjectivity, for example, with nodes of individuality continuously rising and falling on its surface. Each individual would be animated by the Motivating Force. We would see a Planck Code in each individual. We might notice the River of Forgetfulness around the whole scene.

A BHN is not a BHN when you're inside it. It isn't black, it isn't a hole, and it isn't nothing. It's simply the reality on the other side of the River. From within the BHN, we might even try to make out what goes on across the River on the Garden side. We'd probably determine that a so-called "lifetime" of experience in the Garden amounts to an anomalous moment of time in the timeless BHN noxperience. A person's whole life would be a barely noticeable blip in the context of the BHN's silent, timeless domain.

BHN mythology about the Garden (if there were such), would record that "they" (the experiencing individuals across the river: us) believe death is oblivion, but it would be obvious that was just point-of-view bias. Within the BHN, reality is nothing like "death." The experiencing beings "over there" on the Garden side are the odd ones, jumping around like wet beans in a hot frying pan. What are they doing? At least it's quiet in a BHN. Thank goodness for that.

Trouble in BHN

Abiding in a BHN is not peaceful, though. Far from it. A sea of trouble roils. The main difficulties are:

1. Lack of boundaries.

Existence in a BHN is communal because Commodity Subjectivity is undifferentiated. Commodity Subjectivity is not even intersubjective because that involves interaction among individuals, and there are no fully-formed individuals.

2. Boredom.

Another torment for an emerging individual in the BHN would be sheer boredom. Without well-individuated subjectivity, there is no time. Without objectivity, there is no space. Without time or space, nothing can move; nothing can change. The sameness would torment a partially-individuated subjectivity. A potential individual would yearn for change, creativity, even chaos. It would want nothing more than to be in time and embodied in space so it could act.

How BHNs Haunt Experience

Despite being surrounded by the River of Forgetfulness, conditions inside a BHN affect experience here in the Garden. Those effects show up in ordinary experience but may not be recognized for what they are. Here are some examples of such effects.

1. Subjective Tension.

Individual subjectivity (SRS) forming in a BHN never fully detaches from its pre-individual roots in Commodity Subjectivity (CS). The fundamental operation of SRS is to try and purge itself of the self-alien otherness within it. That otherness is really the individual's attachment to the CS field, which it can never get rid of, but it spends a whole lifetime trying to anyway. In that way, the internal dynamics of the BHN condition every aspect of living. We could say death grounds each moment of life.

2. Creative Expression.

Commodity Subjectivity has lower overall energy than the concentrated energy of an individuating node. That energy differential provides a kind of "motivational voltage" that animates the SRS to express itself through intentionality. That energy difference persists throughout life. We might say that death motivates every creative pulse of life.

3. Patterns of Experience.

The Planck Code represents a characteristic pattern of social interaction that could take place in the course of living. The Planck Code in the BHN affects the quality of SRS interactions of self, world, and social engagement. We could say then, that every pattern of living is a pattern of death.

Why We Fear Death

We normally view death as an endpoint to life. I have showed an alternate way of looking at death instead as ongoing juxtapositions to each moment of life. In that view, we see that death plays an essential role in the process of experience. That's possibly a more useful, certainly a more interesting way of thinking about death rather than it being merely a "dead-end" to life.

Conclusion

Having examined the start, middle, and end of death (generalizing over all BHNs), we now have the conceptual tools to take a closer look at life. After all, we live on the Garden-experience side of the River, and our most important questions are about living.

We can ask anew how the rich fullness of self and world come about when we emerge out of a BHN, stripped of everything, naked and bewildered like Botticelli's sea-borne Venus docking her half-shell at a port (Botticelli, ca. 1485)

The Reconstruction

Every day is a new day. When we wake up, the world is largely as we left it but with a glaze of freshness. Anything can happen in a new day. Even in a miserable life, a new day contains a hint of possibility. That's because the world is rebuilt each time we emerge from a BHN, and every rebuild is slightly different. We intuitively recognize that when we appreciate the day's possibilities.

The "Outward Fold," the gradual emergence from a BHN, can be inspected. At the edge of the BHN, where self-awareness is barely a glimmer, one has almost no sense of change. Some Outward Folds are slower and more gradual than others, and in the slow ones, one can watch the bricks being laid in the construction of reality's new edifice. After watching that, it is not as surprising as it first seems that the entirety of self and world is quickly rebuilt after each BHN episode.

In this section, we take a closer look at that process of reconstruction.

Overview of the Reconstruction

The post-BHN reconstruction of self and world, including other people, is called a "*re*construction" not merely a construction, because we assume there was a world prior to the BHN. The new world is a rebuild of it. That's why we tend not to notice BHNs. We mentally patch over the gap caused by the BHN so life seems like a continually unfolding developmental process.

The thesis here is experience is perforated with BHNs, some large, some small. And with each BHN, all is lost: self, relationships, possessions, time, space, ego, personality, achievements, history, the whole world. Nothing is left.

After each BHN, everything must be rebuilt, so I call it the Reconstruction, or Recon for short. Even though you experience only one life, from a Marco Polo point of view, that one life is an episodic Recon, one among uncountable many.

I've already described the critical steps in the process of individuation. Generic, communal, Commodity Subjectivity forms discriminable regions of individual subjectivity of the self-relating kind (SRS). Here, I'll review that process lightly and continue describing the sequence of events out to the full Recon of self and world in order to lay out the sequencing. The steps overlap considerably but the overall order of events is maintained.

The Recon Sequence

Self and world don't suddenly "pop" back after a BHN. It's a process. It's a construction built on foundations, then with superstructure, then with finishes. Here's a summary of the process that emphasizes the sequencing of how it goes.

1. Reconstitution of SRS

First is the formation of an individual subjectivity out of the generic field of Commodity Subjectivity (CS). That's a process called individuation. As described earlier, the individual remains "attached" to the field, but has a boundary that can be identified as "an individual."

The main characteristic of the new individual is that the Planck Code conditions the Motivating Force. In turn, that transforms Commodity Subjectivity into the self-relating kind, SRS, which is capable of supporting mental operations.

2. Establishment of the QMP

Individuated SRS emits vectors of Motivating Force called intentional arcs in an attempt to expel the CS it remains attached to. Each intentional act becomes an objectification of that residual CS. The object is eventually accommodated back to SRS, defining a QMP mental cycle.

3. Development of Community

Self-objects produced by newly-constituted SRS congeal into standalone objects. They constitute objective otherness for SRS. During accommodation, all seemingly external objects, can in principle, be (proto-) recognized as aspects of the subjective self. That's the foundation of intersubjectivity, as we "see" the subjectivity in the other that we feel within ourselves.

4. Physical Instantiation

Full, continued, and robust operation of the QMP requires a medium because individual mentality must be embodied. In all animals, development of an appropriate embodiment for each individual is developed in a collaborative process with the community.

As the process of primary socialization runs, the QMP mental cycle replicates in a process like cellular mitosis. The result is two structurally identical QMP modules. That second module becomes the Sensorimotor Cycle (SMC) module of mind, shown in *Figure 2*.

While purely a mental cycle of activity, the SMC becomes specialized for the non-intellectual mentality of embodiment. Input from the motivational IMS module is re-characterized by the SMC as somatic.

5. Development of Intersubjectivity

Intersubjectivity tacitly acknowledges the CS in which every individual is rooted and from which every object is formed. We somatically feel the presence of our residual CS in ourselves and we apprehend it in the objects of otherness. When CS is objectified into subjective others, a community is formed. Intersubjective social objects "appear" in the mind intuitively as other subjectivities like ourself. They afford a strong sense of self-recognition which becomes intersubjective intuition.

Presence of an intersubjective community first becomes distinct in the form of the primary caregiver, usually the mother. A neonate's sense that mother is "another person, different from me," develops over time. The psychoanalytic literature on this early "splitting" is extensive. At first, there is no mother, just a dimly felt sense of familiar otherness. Then gradually, that mother-other congeals into a discriminable externality for the emerging mind.

The boundary between "me" versus "Mother" is fluid and foggy for many months but gradually resolves into Mother as an intersubjective and embodied not-me other. Complete psychological separation from the mother, if it is ever achieved, may take a lifetime.

Other intersubjective others gradually become apparent to the emerging mind in the same way, and the intersubjective community grows as the individual continues to project self-objects and make discriminations among them. The new individual does not have a pre-existing social community (from a first-person point of view). The individuating mind must intentionally project and objectify its social community.

It's only from the external, third-person, objective point of view that we say, looking back, that the new individual was born "into" a community of others. From the first-person point of view, that is not the case. The community had to be built, one element at a time, like everything else.

Against Solipsism

The suggestion that the social community is an artifact of the individuating entity might seem dehumanizing. If I projected you from my mind, doesn't that rob you of your intrinsic humanity? No. That is an invalid mixture of two points of view called solipsism. It's an error in understanding.

From my individual first-person point of view, you actually *are* a free-standing, independent, intersubjective other, a genuine "not-me." Yet I recognize you. You seem very much like me both physically and subjectively. You are as human as I am from my point of view. You are definitely not me yet I can see myself in you. That paradox of intersubjectivity (not-me, and yet me) is what binds us to other people even while we treat them as self-alien others.

It's only the quasi-fictional, pseudo-omniscient MPM point of view that suggests the idea of others as purely SRS objectifications. No ordinary person has that point of view. If you confuse your actual point of view with an imagined MPM omniscient point of view, you will say incompatible things, and that's solipsism.

This study takes a first-person point of view sometimes filtered through the imaginary MPM point of view. I can do that because I'm the author. It's a narrative technique for purposes of explanation, not a realistic "natural" point of view. It makes no sense in ordinary discourse to say that other people are projections of my mind. Only Marco Polo can say that.

Knowing Others

From the MPM perspective, all other people are indeed reified collaborative projections. Commodity Subjectivity connects everyone prior to their individuation, and after individuation, continues to do so in the new guise of apparently standalone, intersubjective individuals in a contextual community.

For the fully individuated mind, other people have seemingly "always" existed, because that's how reification works. The River of Forgetfulness assures that you do not know what you projected. You take the world as it is because you have no other option.

As a mature mind, we can pause to reflect on the odd fact that we never know another person as they objectively are. You only know someone as you've experienced them, and that's never in full.

We can't explore other people the way we might examine the composition of a mineral down to the last molecule because other people are special objects. Despite their otherness as objects in the world, we also recognize our subjectivity in them as psychological objects. That paradoxical tension goes to the heart of what it means to be an individual person in a community.

That paradox also enables the process of socialization. Other people who are me but not-me can shape my projected self-objects to be increasingly in conformance with tacit community expectations.

The tacit consensus derives from the Commodity Subjectivity, which, in "my" region of the CS field, is constrained by collections of similar Planck Codes. That's why a human is most likely to develop a socialization community of other humans with compatible styles of intersubjective interactions.

6. Furnishing of the Physical World

Rocks seem like total otherness. We hardly recognize any trace subjectivity in them so they do not present the perplexity of intersubjectivity. Nevertheless, each rock was projected from the "substance" of Commodity Subjectivity.

All objects start out as self-objects, and all self-objects are intentional consequences of SRS trying to expel CS. In that sense, the entire world and all its furniture and all its people are ultimately made of communal subjective stuff. However, "ultimately" can only be understood from the alternate reality apprehended by the MPM, not as part of ordinary reality.

Primary socialization is a long process of relentless social learning. Unwittingly, the community instructs each individual about physicality. Physical means explorable by a human body. As awareness of physical embodiment develops, so does the scope of the physical world. Rocks are hard, inert things you can pick up or move (at least the less-than-body-sized ones). So says the community. We believe it.

All the objects of the world are learned one-by-one through painstaking socialization, just as the parts of one's own body were. Primary socializers instruct each child on how the world is constituted, including the properties and capacities of the body, how to behave with other people, and what the community expects of you. And what rocks are, and how they are different from people, and that you shouldn't throw them. Virtually all of that knowledge, of self, other, and world, becomes objectified (reified) into unquestioned and almost unquestionable "objective reality."

7. Ascendance of the Intellect

Along the journey of socialization, as the intersubjective world expands and the physical world is furnished, the individual rational ego grows. A third module of mind, the Socio-linguistic Mind (SLM) splits off to complement the other two, the IMS and SMC. That process starts from the earliest moments of language acquisition. The slow growth of the SLM gets a huge boost with the formation of usable language around age two.

With language, formation of conceptual self-awareness allows the community to teach the individual about the intersubjective community itself. That develops into deepened social empathy, and the "looking-glass self," the sense of how you are seen and understood by others. Along with that explicit intersubjectivity come morality, self-regulation, social cooperation, social judgment, and much else that makes up social life and civilization.

The most dramatic and important development of the SLM occurs in the pre-adolescent period when the SLM discovers itself by introspection. Impressed with itself, the intellect determines that it alone is the entirety of the mind, a self-determined monad of mental agency. Against that, the rest of the world is categorized as external, objective, self-existent, and "not-me." The special case of intersubjective other people remains a lifelong perplexity.

Conclusion

The cosmological Big Bang expanded the universe at a rate of three-hundred-million meters per second. The psychological recreation of first-person self and world ripples into fullness in a few milliseconds after a BHN. Both those world-creations are quicker than the leisurely seven days of the Bible's Genesis story (Genesis 1:1-31). However, we know time is elastic and cannot be assessed by a single standard.

The crucial idea is not how long it takes, but the fact that the world *is* constructed anew after every BHN. Further, the new world is not an exact replica of the prior one. The post-BHN self and world are based on patterns of intersubjectivity held in the Planck Code. They assure that the new world is internally consistent enough that you don't have any reason to suspect it's not your one and only.

But you always come out of a BHN a slightly different person than when you went into it. That's why every morning feels like a new day. It's not just because the birds are singing. It's because you literally are a new person and your world has new possibilities.

The Big Con

In this chapter we entertain the stories of an MPM traveler, an imaginary character who has wandered around inside a BHN with full mentality and self-awareness and has examined the Outward Fold just after. We assume the traveler somehow beat the River of Forgetfulness and is able to report their travel story to us here in the Garden. The purpose of the exercise is to articulate an alternate view of reality.

Our traveler is the opposite of the guy who escaped from Plato's cave, saw the sunshine, and returned to the cave to tell his comrades, "Hey, everybody. There's an entirely different reality out there! What you think is reality is just shadows on the wall." Of course they didn't believe him. Why would they?

Our MPM traveler goes the other way. He, or they, was originally out in the sunshine with us, then ventured into the Black Hole of Nothingness. Then the traveler returned to the bright Garden of ordinary experience and told a strange story. The story is that this world, the sunny one, is (non-cognitively) constructed from our collective minds. Even more incredible, we ourselves are also so constructed.

Do we believe him? Probably not, but now that we have some background on what psychological Black Holes are and what might be in them, we could be more open to the story than Plato's cave-dwellers were to their traveler's tale.

The Big Con

The MPM traveler describes ordinary experience within the Garden as the Big Con. That's short for "Big Construction," another term for what I've described as the Reconstruction or Recon. The reason for the new term is that the traveler is trying to explain our reality *after* it's been built, in terms that ordinary experiencers can appreciate.

In our ordinary view, we interpret reality according to ever-elaborating mental frameworks as we gain more understanding, but we don't consider that a *re*-construction because it's our first time through. We are sure we each have only one life that unfolds in Garden Standard Time, and this is it.

Few of us acknowledge the repeated obliterations and rebuilds of experience in mini- and micro-BHNs and we don't have a reason to think that our life might be a post-demolition rebuild. Out of respect for that Garden-standard view, the MPM traveler calls the world the Big Construction, or Big Con. The term acknowledges that the world presents as "given."

The term "Big Con" also connotes something fishy, as if it were a confidence trick, as if reality were an illusion or delusion. That's a deniable implication. I don't mean it that way. The idea that life as we experience it is illusory or delusional, unreal, or somehow not what it seems to be, has little basis within the walls of ordinary experience. Inside the Garden, everything adds up. Only an outsider can see the anomalies.

Anomalies

What anomalies? Some inconsistent elements of ordinary reality that the MPM traveler notes about the Big Con include:

Individualism

Each of us believes we are purely an individual. But we live in neverending confusions about empathy, morality, love, and other intersubjective relations.

The Objective World

Our consensus belief is that the objective world is self-existent, "external" and unaffected by human minds current or past. But we also understand that if the world were literally made of mind-independent "matter," it could have no possible interface to mentality, and we would never know about it.

History

The main reason we believe the world is mind-independent and self-existent is that we are sure it preceded mentality. In our usual telling of history, the inorganic world came first, then life evolved, and consciousness came along only recently. At the same time, we recognize that history is a retrospective intellectual construction that inevitably tends to justify current beliefs. "What happened" is a campfire story, yet we believe our histories literally.

Stream of Consciousness

Most of us would characterize consciousness as a flow of continuous life-experience, even allowing for unexplained brief interruptions here and there by sleep, anesthesia or concussions. Yet accessible BHNs prove that experience is "bursty," not continuous, and suggests that mentality itself is quantized. We unwittingly patch over the innumerable blind spots in experience to create a story of continuity.

Death

Most of us believe that death is the terminus of life, a singularity and a journey of no return into oblivion. But there are sound reasons to think that death is just another BHN, and like all BHNs, terminates, and is followed by a Reconstruction.

This short list is only illustrative. Many other anomalies in the standard story of reality can be enumerated, including accounts of growth, development, and aging; the meaning of science and mathematics; the definitions of life and consciousness; the separation of subjectivity from objectivity;

the nature of embodiment; the reality of time; the mechanisms of memory; quantum entanglement, and many others. The careful reader of this essay will be able to generate a long inventory of cracks in the Garden walls.

Who is Right?

Billions of people in the world hold the Garden-variety beliefs. Should we take seriously a handful of oddball MPM travelers who declare that reality is not what it seems? Yes and no. We can entertain both points of view, just not at the same time.

The two views, that of the MPM traveler and that of the ordinary Garden-dweller, are not incompatible because they're not concurrent. They are alternating and sequential. They oscillate. That's how they don't contradict each other.

It's only the fiction of the MPM traveler that lets us take a pseudo-omniscient point of view to regard both sides of the Garden wall at once. In ordinary experience we only know what we know, constrained by what we believe. We have no other perspective normally. The device of the MPM traveler provides another perspective if you can wrap your mind around it.

The MPM traveler frolics in Otherland and returns (outsmarting the River) to describe the Big Con to those of us inside the Walled Garden of ordinary experience. The traveler is never in both places at once. Inside the Garden, the MPM traveler's stories can be dismissed as fictional nonsense. Or, they could be taken seriously by someone interested in an alternative point of view.

Other MPM Travelers

Plenty of MPM travelers have reported alternate descriptions of ordinary reality similar to what is described in this essay. Those are descriptions of Otherland, the world of noxperience inside the BHNs that perforate everyday life. Other travelers use their own language and images, of course.

Italo Calvino's novella, *Invisible Cities*, describes in fictional language what Otherland looks like. In mythical language, so does the *Bible*, in Genesis and in other sections. Early Greek philosophy and mythology are great sources of quasi-fictional information about Otherland, as are many myths and legends from around the world. Greek, Hindu, and Buddhist philosophies, among others, describe alternate domains of reality similar to my account of Otherland.

A recent philosopher who describes a similar reality of "otherness" is Gilbert Simondon (2020; and cited by Grosz, 2017 and Combes, 2013). His ideas have been noted previously in this essay and are currently being translated into English. He is an influential precursor to philosopher Gilles Deleuze, currently in vogue. I'll take a moment therefore to compare Simondon's idea of pre-individual reality to the process of post-BHN reconstruction that results in the Big Con.

Simondon's Pre-individual Reality

My account of the individuation of SRS from Communal Subjectivity in the BHN and of the Reconstruction in the post-BHN Outward Fold agree with Simondon's descriptions in several ways, although we use different language and begin with different assumptions. Here are some examples of agreement.

Fungibility of Time

Simondon says that the individual "carries with it" all the processes that created it. Because of that, "past is present." (From Grosz, 2017). I say something similar because every thought comes out of the accommodative BHN as a reconstruction of all of life leading up to that moment. All of the past is thus contained in every present moment, even though we only see the present.

I also propose that the Planck Code is a continually updated repository of essential intersubjective features of life-experience, again assuring that "the past is the present." Simondon and I agree (along with Bergson, 1889), that psychological time is a different phenomenon than clock time.

The Impersonal Preindividual

According to Simondon, every individual started out in a pre-individual reality, which he calls simply "the preindividual" (From Grosz, 2017). I call that preindividual the field of Commodity Subjectivity (CS). We agree that the preindividual condition has no cognitive content. It participates in no mentality. Simondon emphasizes that it is not composed of "things." That implies it must be a field. I agree.

Invoking ideas from chaos theory, Simondon says individuals "self-organize" out of the preindividual field at points where a foreign "seed" nucleates it. I suggest something similar with my description of the Planck Code as a persistent "seed" derived from pre-BHN experience. The presence of the Planck Code nucleates the process of individuation from the CS.

I don't subscribe to chaos theory or even to the idea of autopoiesis as Simondon does, but we do agree that the preindividual field is not personal. What provokes individuality out of the non-individual is the presence of a local externality, which is the Planck Code in my account.

Persistence of the Preindividual

Even after formation of the individual (a process called individuation), the individual continues to hold a preindividual residual, according to Simondon. I concur. I say that individual subjectivity remains inextricably rooted in the preindividual CS from which it arose.

Both Simondon and I say that an individual person is not aware of its residual preindividual roots but the ongoing tension between individual and preindividual nevertheless creates intrinsic tension (Simondon calls it "anxiety") in the forever-unstable individual (He calls it a "metastable" condition). That fits my description of the individuated SRS which is always internally torn between self and other.

I go on to account for the individual having no memory or concept of the residual CS that torments it because of the metaphorical River of Forgetfulness, or in more prosaic terms, the amnesia of reification. Simondon does not explain the amnesia or indeed, give any role to subjectivity in individuation. He's an objectophile.

Individual Motivation

Simondon says that the individual, acts to "expand" itself in an attempt to reduce internal anxiety. He seems to take the idea of expansion quite literally and goes into a great deal of detail about the growth of crystals from a supersaturated solution. The idea seems to be that a physically "larger" individual would somehow overcome the relatively small preindividual component causing all the trouble.

I take the idea of expansion less literally, as the repeated and cumulating updating of the Planck Code. That update resets the boundaries of SRS subjectivity to (metaphorically) include more of the objective domain. Phenomenologically, the mature mind feels "expanded" when the world is better understood. While Simondon and I agree in principle that the individual acts to "expand" itself, we mean different things by that expression.

Does individual "expansion" reduce "anxiety?" For me, yes. The SRS acts to rid itself of its felt otherness. That defines its motivational telos. To the extent that each QMP cycle is successful, a "positive" update results for the Planck Code. It's not "anxiety-reduction" in the ego-sense, but rather, a subjective "move" toward wholeness and unity that reduces the ever-present alienation between "me" and "not-me." Simondon is less clear about the mechanics of motivation.

Differences

While we agree on several key ideas, Simondon and I diverge on many points. Here are a few, for the purpose of clarifying my ideas.

The Individual

Most fundamentally, we differ on what counts as an individual. I say that immediately prior to individuation, a particular region in the impersonal field of Commodity Subjectivity develops a bulb of Self-relating subjectivity (SRS). It's an individual because it has a boundary that defines inner from outer, individual subjectivity from generic subjectivity.

Simondon defines the individual as a self-organizing object in the preindividual field but fails to specify who the subject is. His approach privileges ontology over epistemology, the opposite of my approach. He can name objects without any reference to who does the naming because the subject (himself) is invisible to his theory. That's the basic flaw of any ontology-first argument.

Physicality

Simondon implicitly defines an object as a physical object. He eschews Cartesian substance dualism, as I do, but all his examples of individuality seem to presuppose that they are physical objects. His fixation on crystals and their growth as the exemplar of individuation supports that inference.

By contrast, my account of individuation is entirely non-physical. Individuals are bounded regions of subjectivity formed out of a larger field of commodity subjectivity. Physicality arises much later in development as reified self-projections explorable by a bodily SMC mentality.

Vitalism

Simondon believes the membrane that defines the boundary of an individual constitutes life (cited in Grosz, 2017). He does not define what he thinks life is, but he seems to take the idea of "membrane" quite literally, drawing analogies to the biological cell membrane. For him, the difference between an interiority and an exteriority is enough to define life. Since individuation involves boundary formation, that makes Simondon essentially a pan-vitalist. In this, his thinking seems to run much closer to Bergson's than mine does.

Simondon says life arises from the internal tension between the individual and its residual preindividual condition. I concur with the presence of such a tension. "Technical objects," he calls them, do not involve the same internal tension as "live" objects. Similarly, I say that brute objects are not self-relating and therefore not subject to internal tension.

But none of that has much to do with "life." Objectivity, for me, is the difference between the self-relating form of existence that constitutes the subjective individual and the brute (unknowing, non-self-relating) existence of its juxtaposed objects.

Because he's an ontologist, Simondon sees everything as "objective." Therefore, mere interaction among objects ("resonance," he cryptically calls it) is proof of life. But for me, resonance is something tuning forks do. It's passive, unmotivated, and uninteresting. It does not sound sufficient for defining life, which is driven by motivated subjectivity.

I don't have a definition of life. That's a biological question for others to deal with. I am concerned with the formation of a subjective individual out of Commodity Subjectivity, and after that, formation of full individual mentality.

I say subjectivity is active, motivated, anti-entropically developmental, and it eventually leads to the Big Con of a populated and furnished world. I don't think the concept of "life" is essential or even useful for a discussion of early individuation.

The Transindividual

Simondon's concept of the transindividual (TI) does not map well to my ideas. The TI for him seems to be a mix of intersubjectivity and a re-entry into the preindividual state. At death, he says, one renounces all identity, personality, and personal qualities (Grosz, 2017, p. 196). On that much we agree. But Simondon says that after such "dis-individuation," one partakes in the TI, a different kind of becoming. He's unclear (to me, at least) about what that state is.

In my view, at death, one enters the "big" BHN, but it's no different in principle than any other BHN. With loss of virtually all traces of individuality, nothing personal is left.

Entry into the BHN is shedding the trappings of individuation and going back to the beginning. And that beginning cannot involve anything like intersubjectivity because there's no "individual" left.

Simondon says that the TI is a sort of communal, interpersonal state from which art arises. It seems to me he is talking about intersubjectivity. It looks to me as if Simondon's transindividual state is a conflation of individual with the pre-individual. The are not unrelated, but he fails to draw a clear distinction.

In my view, during the heart of each intersubjective transaction, each individual momentarily gives up their individuality and metaphorically takes the other person's point of view. That's what it means to understand someone. That's the "holiness" of Buber's I-Thou relationship. But giving up one's individuality is also tantamount to death. One voluntarily "dies" for the other and is reborn an instant later. That happens during every intersubjective moment.

However, at no point is there a new condition that could be called a "transindividual." Intersubjective understanding is individual. Commodity Subjectivity isn't. After a BHN, the former might get an intuitive glimpse of the latter. As with all creativity, art is an insight about one's constitution, not a transcendence of it.

As an object-oriented ontologist, Simondon omits subjectivity from reality almost entirely, so he cannot have a concept like intersubjectivity. For him, the fact of intersubjective experience must be expressed as transcendent objectivity, an idea I find unsatisfactory and contrary to experience. Furthermore, omitting subjectivity deprives Simondon's system of any concept of the Outward Fold during which the Big Con is rebuilt and which offers epistemological access to the Recon process.

Reification

My own view of objectivity depends on the concept of psychological reification. Most definitions of reification describe it as the practice of using an abstract concept as if it were a concrete entity.

A typical reification might produce the claim that Nature abhors a vacuum. What we mean is that in nature, vacuums fill very quickly, *as if* Nature were a personality that abhorred them. It's merely a colorful, metaphorical way of speaking or writing.

In a psychological reification, however, the speaker "forgets" that it's a metaphor and actually believes that the reified (concretized) entity is objectively self-existent. For example, we see that people do evil things, so we abstract the concept of evil as if it were something that literally exists in nature. "Evil" then becomes the source of evil deeds. It's an objective entity "out there."

The person who has reified evil this way has "forgotten" that it started out as a generalized abstraction and now believes wholeheartedly in Evil as a concrete and even personified "presence." That happens when the abstraction is accompanied by amnesia about its origins.

Reification is how we get Evil, Lady Luck, Fate, gods and devils, and much else. Reification is generally taken to be an error in thinking.

With the idea of the Big Con, I generalize the process of psychological reification to all of objective reality. Subjectivity projects "otherness-objects," or self-objects in each act of intentionality, then "forgets" that it did, and then encounters the objects "out there" as the self-existent furniture of the world. If subjectivity were a mind (which it isn't) it would be a realist, believing that the reified objective domain was simply the "given" reality.

Reality is mind-independent if you have amnesia about where it came from. That's exactly what happens in the Big Con. (I am not immune to the irony that I have come very close to reifying the concept of the Big Con.)

Solipsism and Realism

Despite a process that generates objective reality from mentality, the Big Con does not constitute solipsism. I cannot say this enough times. The Recon regenerates self and world tacitly, in collaboration with the concurrently emerging community. The world is not something one individual dreams up, which is the view of solipsism.

Everybody's involved in the Recon. Primary socialization is a very collaborative process. It takes a village to raise each individual, plus the individual's eager participation. It's not solipsism if everybody's in on it.

Also, virtually none of the Recon is cognitive. The world is already about 75% built (just to put a number on it) before the intellectual module of the mind even becomes fully functional around age two. By that time, traces of the construction process are long-since erased by the River of Forgetfulness. So it is flatly incorrect to say that the Recon is a solipsism or even an idealism. Even "projection," a term I use often, sounds like a cognitive act, but it isn't.

"Reality," as commonly understood by the mature mind, is object-oriented realism, not an explicit mental projection of any kind. From the point of view of ordinary, well-socialized consciousness, reality is not an illusion, delusion, or simulation. Reality is as real as real can get. As a person who lives in the Garden, I am not arguing for any kind of anti-realism or idealism. The world exists; it exists physically; it exists mind-independently.

It is only the fictional MPM traveler who says "Realism, sure, but where do you think all that mind-independent reality *came from*?" The traveler questions the *origins* of realism. But unless you are that traveler, the origins are unquestionable and realism is given.

Of course, metaphysical dogmatists (and most scientists) insist that a "real realist" must singlemindedly believe in the objective, mind-independent, self-existent, "material" world. Entertain even a whisper of doubt about that and one is an "anti-realist." But that kind of unquestioning realism is not a scientific principle. It's not philosophically plausible. It's not even reasonable. It's an article of faith that withstands epistemology. I encourage readers to exercise more imagination to engage the MPM traveler.

Why Does Life End So Badly?

We hate loss. We don't like losing our stuff. We cringe at losing social status. We suffer badly when we lose loved ones. We panic at losing mental capacity. We despair at the loss of memories and meaning. And above all, we hate losing bodily integrity and functionality, which usually involves pain, which we especially hate. All loss is suffering.

Entry into the BHN of death is big-time loss of everything. It therefore necessarily involves great suffering. Does it have to be that way? Buddha said no. If you didn't cling to life (desire it) so much, loss of it would not cause you to suffer. If you give up your attachment to something, it doesn't matter if you lose it. If it doesn't matter, no suffering occurs at the prospect of its loss or with its actual loss.

That may seem a bit glib for most of us who cling to life. We cling to life because it is the only way of being we've ever known. Constructed or not, life is life, and oblivion is nothingness. So call us clingy if you will, O Buddha. That's where most of us are "at."

We might wonder why, if from the point of view of the MPM traveler, life is a construction built collaboratively by each individual and their community, does it end unhappily. Why couldn't the Inward Fold to the BHN of death be more gentle? Why does it have to involve pain, loss, and suffering? Nobody prefers that. Couldn't the individual and the community come up with a better ending?

It kind of did. Buddhist philosophy does exist. You can read it and choose to believe it. Christianity and other religions have their stories. Even so, rare is the person who faces the relentless and increasingly severe losses of old age with equanimity.

We cling because we *must* believe in the unquestionable givenness of our bodies and the world. We *need* them to appear as self-existent givens, objective facts, not any kind of mental constructs. Why? Because biological uniqueness in space, time, and community guarantees psychological individuality. Without psychological individuality we would flow into each other and become a featureless subjective soup. That's a fair way to describe Commodity Subjectivity.

We absolutely must have hard-shell, individual, separate, objective bodies in an objectively "given" world in order to be the intersubjective beings that we are. The Reconstruction is a slick system that provides just what's needed. But on the down side, the bodies and their world are so robust that the system only comes apart at the end with great difficulty. And loss. And suffering.

The reconstruction may be over-engineered for psychological safety. A less robust belief in unique, self-existent bodies and the world would dissolve more gently and easily at the end. But then, one's reflective psyche might also have frightening questions about its identity at awkward moments after life's many smaller BHNs.

Conclusion

The Big Con is a deeper account of realism. It's a propadeutic or precursor that makes belief in realism possible.

Once the Big Con is built, reality is a reified "given." But if you look behind the curtain at how it got built, that alters your perception of what you see in front of the curtain. Importantly, it also alters your idea of what's possible.

Imagination plays a part in appreciating the MPM traveler's story. We need to suspend our disbelief as we do when we appreciate any work of fiction. In that mode of cognition, we can temporarily oscillate into the traveler's viewpoint and see the reality of our world in a different light. Assuming the reader can do that without too much trouble, I'll exploit that quasi-fictional space explore the final aspect of death as a BHN: the possibility of reincarnation.

Reincarnation

Carne means flesh, derived from the Latin. "Carne Asada" is a grilled meat dish. A carnation is a flower in various flesh-tones centered around pink. A Spanish butcher shop is a carnicería. Chile con carne has meat in it.

From etymology, it's easy to imagine that "to carnate" could be a verb. I don't think it's really a word, but if it was, it would mean "to become flesh." "Carnation," used as a verb is the *process* of flesh-forming. That's what we do when we're born. We undergo in-carnation, coming *into* the flesh. Do it again, and you have *re*-incarnated.

Reincarnation is the idea that some aspect of each person continues to exist after death of its body, and the surviving aspect subsequently acquires a new body. It "incarnates" again.

Definitions

The doctrine of reincarnation focuses on "carnation," the flesh, to the virtual exclusion of all other considerations. That leads to deep confusion that's almost impossible to sort out. For example, the online *Cambridge Dictionary* defines reincarnation as:

"..the belief that the spirit of a dead person returns to life in another body."

What is "the spirit of a dead person?" Do dead people *have* spirits? Is a dead body even a "person?"

If it's the spirit that makes the body alive, then the definition is backward: the spirit does *not* return to life, the body does. But wait, it says *another* body returns to life, not the one that just died. If the dead body just got up and walked again, that would be resurrection, not reincarnation.

So the escaped spirit must find a different body, presumably a dead one, otherwise, you'd have the awkward situation of a body with two spirits. So reincarnation seems to be about re-animation of corpses. It sounds like a horror movie.

The doctrine of reincarnation, when stated so badly, is an easy target of ridicule. Maybe we can do better. The basic idea is that the supernatural soul does not perish with the body, but "moves" (metaphorical movement, for souls are not physical) into an about-to-be-born baby or other animal that has not yet acquired a body. *Transmigration,* or reincarnation, is accomplished when the soul has inhabited the new body.

It's not clear if the newborn animal would have acquired a soul anyway, or if reincarnation is its only source of soul. If souls can only come from reincarnation, relentless population growth would create an increasingly severe shortage of souls when more people are born than die. The result would be lot of people without souls. I think I worked for a boss like that once. But that's a divergent line of thought. It's best not to question the doctrine too closely.

Reincarnation is widely accepted by many major religions, notably Hinduism and Buddhism. It was prominent in ancient Greek philosophy and with the ancient Druids and Celts, according to Roman records. Earliest textual references to reincarnation are in the *Upanishads* of India (c. 800 BCE). Reincarnation does not feature in the mainstream Abrahamic religions.

This essay takes a naturalistic approach, working only with entities and processes that can be observed or inferred from observation. That rules out souls.

However, I have proposed some elements of mentality that survive the loss of the body, namely, Commodity Subjectivity, the Planck Code, and the Motivating Force. With those, re-incarnation could be a possibility worth considering.

We assume death is a BHN like other BHNs except for the fact that we have no experience of its Outward Fold. Nevertheless, by analogy, the BHN of death should terminate and be followed by a period of Reconstruction based on persistent trans-BHN entities.

Looking at the main principles and processes operating in and around a BHN, parallels to the doctrine of reincarnation are apparent. Despite its religious roots and implications, reincarnation is a set of ideas worth looking at.

Embodiment vs Individuation

An important distinction is between embodiment and individuation. The Reconstruction after a BHN begins with subjective individuation out of the generic subjective field. Embodiment comes much later.

Reincarnation is all about getting a new body, but that's a downstream detail. Individuation of subjectivity is the first job to be accomplished after termination of a BHN. That has nothing to do with reincarnation.

Individuation is a process of subjectivity, not corporeality. A motivationally charged field of Commodity Subjectivity develops a "bubble" on its surface. A bubble has a boundary that distinguishes it from the rest of the field and from any other bubbles. The bubble swells into a bulb, concentrating Motivating Force in a defined region to form self-relating subjectivity, SRS, the individual kind.

From the BHN's point of view (if it had one, which it doesn't), the field of Commodity Subjectivity is not exhausted by the process and carries on after individuation. Only the Marco Polo Method (MPM) of description lets us imagine "what it is like" to be there and watch an individual subjectivity be born out of the commodity field.

Birth and Rebirth

I have defined "birth" of the individual as subjective individuation leading to establishment of the Quantum Mental Process (QMP). In traditional accounts of reincarnation, that step is skipped and the transmigrating soul simply "takes up" a new body. But how is that supposed to work?

We know where new bodies come from. For us, it involves sex. Just how the transmigrating soul is supposed to weasel itself into the sex act is omitted from most teachings on reincarnation.

One interesting exception though is pictorial. Many ancient temples in India are covered in multitudes of detailed carvings of explicit human sexual acts. They are surprising and fascinating for the Western traveler, but they're not there for titillation. They are instructional, which is why they're on the walls of religious buildings.

The carvings are often described in travelers' guidebooks as "erotic," but that is a complete misunderstanding. The images are to be meditated upon. Doing that leads you mentally into the sex scene shown—not as one of the participants depicted, but beyond that, to the psychological and spiritual essence of sexuality. That is similar to how a transmigrating soul gets in on the act, so to speak. The images are like an ancient training video for embodiment-seeking souls.

Does it work? Sort of. If you meditate on the psychological essence of sexual intercourse, what do you find? A Black Hole of Nothingness. Orgasm has often been described as "the little death" because at the moment of sexual climax, one temporarily loses one's self-awareness. That's the BHN that a body-seeking soul must find and occupy. That BHN is the portal to its new embodied life.

The orgasm story is largely a male-centric description of sexuality, but even without an orgasm, BHNs are frequent in the human mind. Each moment of intersubjective intimacy involves two BHNs. There's plenty of opportunity for transmigrating souls to occupy one.

Of the two potential parents, which one's BHNs should the embodiment-seeking soul choose? One wants to say the female's but since BHNs are not gendered (the physical body having perished), the question is an error in point of view.

Maybe the whole "training video" approach to soul-instruction is an error, when you think about it. The soul is supposed to be unembodied, not standing around watching physical sex as if it were a person. But maybe that insight is part of the exercise: to discriminate embodied from unembodied subjectivity and intersubjectivity.

All descriptions of reincarnation are offered by the embodied, to the embodied, for the embodied. They're understandably biased toward physicality. Traditional writings on reincarnation imagine a self-aware, transmigrating spirit with a determined point of view, desperately trying to get reborn by stealthily inserting itself into a human sexual act. But that image is strictly an embodied person's fantasy.

Nearly all descriptions of reincarnation are fantastical and confused. It's understandable, considering life in the Garden of ordinary experience. Even so, just as we can learn things from interpreting a crazy dream, we can benefit from contemplating traditional accounts of reincarnation.

Your New Body

Reincarnation is not resurrection. With reincarnation, you get a whole new body, presumably a young one that gives you a chance for a long life. What kind of body do you get? In Eastern traditions, that depends on your karma. According to the *Upanishads* and the *Tibetan Book of the Dead*, the possibilities include "coming back" as:

A hungry ghost

This is a reincarnation that didn't quite "take." Ghosts have only "subtle" bodies, not fleshy ones. The embodiment procedure apparently did not go well. That explains why ghosts appear as filmy, undulating apparitions in alleged photographs of them. This semi-carnation supposedly happens if you have "clingy" karma and can't let go of your previous life. You can't have two bodies, so if you can't give up your old life, you're not going to get a new one, and you're stuck in the middle as a ghost.

An animal

At least an animal has a solid, physical body made of meat, so it's a transmigration that went to completion. On the downside, for a human, it's a nonhuman animal, and presumably, nobody wants that. Animals lack the capacity for advanced socio-linguistic cognition, reflective self-awareness, and articulated intersubjectivity. Some older texts say this category of reincarnation includes plants also.

As a human, reincarnating as a plant or an animal would be "going backward" on your journey to "liberation" from the cycle of reincarnation. Such regression is caused by really bad karma that canceled whatever good karma you had accumulated. It seems that if you had made it all the way to being a human, you would have banked a lot of good karma that should prevent backsliding, but apparently not. If you were a particularly evil person, your karmic balance could tip into the red.

Not considered in traditional accounts is the possibility that a person might enjoy reincarnation as a non-human animal. One can imagine a long, rich, and interesting life at sea as a whale, for example, or the exhilarating hunting life of an eagle. Even the quiet life of an oak tree might be appealing to some. Of course that's all anthropomorphic fantasy. We don't really know "what it's like" to be a whale or an eagle. Still, human life is fraught with miseries, so who's to say other kinds of embodiment are less good?

A human

Most of us presumably would want, and would get a human body again. What kind of a new human body could you acquire? A young one for sure, one not yet separated from its womb. Beyond that, the kind of body would be determined by your karmic situation, though the scriptures are surprisingly evasive on how karma actually determines the specific incarnation.

One reasonable account says your karma does not directly determine the kind of body, but rather, the kind of family. Good karma will get you a "good" family, meaning virtuous and prosperous. The actual physical body is determined by family genetics in the usual way. That's about all the detail on human embodiment to be had from traditional descriptions.

God or Demigod

If you have super-duper good karma, you can be reborn as a god or demigod. Some texts lump those together—they're all gods. Others fractionate the category into two dozen subtypes of demigod. But as any kind of god, the texts say, you don't have to work, yet you can enjoy all the pleasures of heaven and earth. The texts are vague on details.

If earthly pleasures include beer and pizza, even a demigod would require a fleshy body. Heavenly pleasures, whatever they might be, presumably do not require a meat package. Regardless, the texts say that pleasure of any kind brings attachment, and attachment leads to loss, and loss causes suffering, and suffering accumulates more karma. So even as a god, you have to be quite cautious about pleasure. Inattention could unwittingly drop you back into the karmic cycle of physical embodiment.

It first seems as if being lightly embodied as a god would be a good thing, but upon closer examination, it looks like prudence would still dictate a life of anhedonia (no pleasure). Offsetting that, there would be no work. Is that a good trade-off? I'm not sure. Looking at the range of antics of mythical Greek and Roman gods, they couldn't decide either. Some (such as Dionysus) embraced the earthly pleasures wholeheartedly, while others (such as Apollo) eschewed them. Zeus seemed ambivalent.

Carnation and Individuality

I treat these Eastern descriptions of reincarnation lightly, not out of disrespect, but because in my way of thinking, reincarnation is not mainly about embodiment at all. Carnation is a red herring or at least a red flower. Reincarnation is really about replaying the trajectory of psychological individuation. The traditional descriptions of reincarnation get side-tracked by obsession with physical bodies.

Biology is our story of a complex system of life that meets our psychological needs. We have the kind of bodies that let us live the kind of life we have imagined. But there's nothing special about biology. Embodiment in silicon or information nets could work just as well as long as they supported our subjectivity, mentality, and consciousness. That's what's important about us. It hardly matters what kind of a body you get upon reincarnation as long as you get the right mind.

Once embodied, the next big challenge is the post-embodiment process of social teaching and learning which sustains the belief that you are an individual.

Beyond Reincarnation

The doctrine of reincarnation offers a prospect of return from death, and if true, would make death more consistent with the other BHNs. However, the evidence and reasoning supporting reincarnation are not compelling. The doctrine doesn't even seem to address the main problem.

"Carnation," that is, embodiment, is not the main challenge to a post-BHN Reconstruction. Rather, it is re-individuation, formation of a new individual subjectivity out of generic and communal Commodity Subjectivity.

I have described the process of subjective individuation in some detail already. Here, I extend that process specifically to the context of "recovery" from death, if there is such a thing, which there should be if death is just another BHN. I call that extended process *Reindeering.*

Reindeering

Reindeering is the early process of individuation that precedes socialization. It involves individual SRS formation from Commodity Subjectivity, followed by the Reconstruction of self, community and world. It's only later in the Recon process that socialization begins. That's where the primary caregivers, starting even as far back as conversation between the future parents, begin interacting with the anticipated and then newly-individuated SRS to continue rebuilding that individual's self and world. Primary socialization is well-documented in the psychological literature, but Reindeering occurs before that and is neglected. In this section, Reindeering is contrasted to the idea of reincarnation.

Why You Will Not Reincarnate as a Squirrel

"Reindeer" derives from a strained acronym: **Re-ind**ividuation & **E**mpathic **E**nvironment **R**econstruction. We've described the early stages of Re-individuation of SRS subjectivity from Commodity Subjectivity. What about the rest of the acronym, the Empathic Environment Reconstruction? That's the aspect of the earliest individuation process that assures the individual's reconstituted social community is appropriate. It assures that if you go to sleep as a person, you won't wake up as a squirrel.

A squirrel is a conscious, individual animal that lives in a squirrel community located in a squirrel reality that makes sense to squirrels. There's nothing wrong with being a squirrel. Except we don't really want to be one. But what prevents it? If all the world is lost upon going into a BHN, and all the world is rebuilt "from scratch" upon coming out of a BHN, what's to prevent your new world from being squirrel-world?

Constraints

Three factors operate in the early Reindeering process to constrain the Reconstruction to what is appropriate for the newly-emerged SRS. One is the state the CS field when "you" enter the BHN. The other is the condition of the Planck Code when you leave it.

A. Entering the BHN

We imagine the undifferentiated field of Commodity Subjectivity as a surface undulating with the excess energy of undifferentiated Motivational Force. Local bulbs of individuating subjectivity rise and fall from the surface like hot air balloons. (In Marco Polo's imagination. See Figure 5).

A person enters a BHN as a non-person. When falling asleep, for example, your self, your world, and finally your body gradually "evaporate" until there's nothing left of you to support a first-person perspective. That's the nothingness of the BHN of sleep. It's not even "black." It's not really "a hole." It's not even nothing. It is the absence of the first-person point of view and everything juxtaposed to it.

Despite that first-person oblivion, a third-person (MPM) point of view says that three non-personal mental elements survive and persist. They are Commodity Subjectivity, the Motivational Force, and the Planck Code.

B. Perturbing the Field

The Planck Code acts as an irritant or stimulant on the field of Commodity Subjectivity. That occasions the formation of a new individual at that spot. Why that spot and not some other? (These are MPM metaphorical spaces). Is the location random?

A perturbation at location (x,y) on the CS surface will tend to reoccur where it has before. Just as individual sinkholes tend to persist and reoccur at certain spots on a roadway, and rashes erupt at the same location on one's body over time, and weather events tend to follow the same patterns every year, and migrating birds stop at the same locations, there is a certain reliable rhythm to Planck Code nucleation on a CS field.

The idea that new individuals tend to precipitate at reoccurring locations suggests a kind of morphogenic field, analogous perhaps to the common cultural belief in sacred places. What would cause re-individuation to occur repeatedly in certain regions of the CS surface? My best guess is that it's related to affinity among similar Planck Codes that are already re-individuating at that spot.

We can suppose that similar Planck Codes cluster in regions of the CS field, forming pre-individual, very early communal conditions for future individuals of a similar type. The likelihood of a squirrel's Planck Code (assuming they have one), getting mixed up in a cluster of human Planck Codes on the CS surface would be low.

Likewise, we would not expect a (pre-BHN) person with a Planck Code of type A (however defined), to end up on the CS field among a cluster of Type Z Planck Codes. Because the Planck Code defines the nature of relationships between individuals and communities, we would expect it to be affected by the relationship between local energy conditions on the communal CS surface and the kind of Planck Codes already in that region. They would have affinity.

If that reasonable speculation is accurate, your chances of individuating into a world and a culture radically different from the one you left are remote. The chance that you will emerge as a squirrel is even more remote. Kafka's cockroach notwithstanding, we need not worry about bizarre reincarnation scenarios.

C. Condition of the Planck Code

Another factor contributing to harmony between neo-individual and community post-BHN is the ongoing evolution of each individual's Planck Code. If the condition of a Planck Code upon arriving at the CS field is crucial to the outcome, we need to consider how the Planck Code acquired its condition.

The Planck Code contains information from all your previous intersubjective acts, including the valence and strength of satisfaction from each mental cycle.

All the world (including one's body) is "made of" subjectively-projected otherness, and all otherness is ultimately made of Commodity Subjectivity. Therefore, every mental confrontation with any object is an intersubjective act in principle, though not understood that way throughout the personal realm of experience.

The intersubjective content of an interaction is more apparent in some cases than others. Our intersubjective "sense" is fairly crude. Some people struggle to recognize the humanity of even ordinary other people. We easily "dehumanize" or objectify members of other tribes.

However, most of us can recognize the SRS of other people readily and even feel co-subjective with a dog. Maybe a squirrel. Possibly a spider. But not a rock. It's not a perfect system.

The Planck Code contains the cumulative result of a lifetime's intersubjective acts. That cumulated content is the key factor determining what *kind* of individual and what *kind* of world emerges from the CS field. It would be manifest in the mature adult mind as intersubjective sensitivity.

Re-individuation (and reincarnation) are not random, but neither are they personal choices as suggested in Plato's story, *The Myth of Er*. Rather, the Recon is a personally-impersonal formulation constrained by the information in the Planck Code, and the information in the Planck Code is qualitatively intersubjective.

The Parameters of Goodness

Each successful accommodation of an object is positive. Positive accommodations absorb a bit of otherness back into the subjective domain, expanding the footprint of SRS, making the world more familiar.

Intersubjective objects are more readily recognizable as intersubjective objects and thus produce more satisfaction. A Planck Code filled with neutral or negative outcomes would not be as likely to produce positive accommodations in the future. A Planck Code from a highly sensitive intersubjective person would promise a strongly intersubjectively tinged Recon.

A Planck Code derived from mostly successful intersubjective accommodations leads to more possibilities for positive action in the future. The number of different kinds of satisfactory future Big Con realities becomes greater with every experience of positive intersubjective experience in this, the current Big Con.

In the language of reincarnation, we could say the next incarnation will have more possibilities for satisfaction if you already have a ton of good karma. There will be more situations that could meet your needs. With less good karma, the options for an excellent reincarnation are fewer and you could even end up in a near-identical replay of the last cycle.

In sum, the Planck Code determines the intersubjective degrees of freedom available in the Recon.

Coming Into a Good Family

Typically, the kernel of a new socialization community is one's family. Family is constructed along with everything else as part of the Recon. What counts as a good family for you is determined in your Planck Code from your past experience with your community. A new family is constructed to be compatible with the intersubjective traits already represented in the Planck Code.

Once constructed, your new family provides the right kind of empathic environment for you to optimize positive social interactions. That in turn lets you develop into a personality with temperaments and abilities suitable to your Planck Code and which will, over time, increase your life-satisfaction in a positive feedback cycle. That empathic environment reconstruction is the EER in Reindeer.

Your presence in a community also modifies the community. Each person interacting with others defines the quality of the whole network in every pulse of consciousness. That's how you do your part to shape the community you need even as it shapes you into the individual it wants.

Bad Family

But what if you hate your family, your social status, the world, and even your body? If you could articulate it, you'd say your current Big Con sucks.

That matters, but not as much as you might think. The "rightness" of fit between your Planck Code and your Reconstructed Big Con is defined by your intersubjective history, not by your intellect, social status, circumstances, or personal preferences. It doesn't really matter what you think about your lot in life.

The machinations of Reindeering and early socialization occur long before formation of the self-aware, tripartite mind. By the time you understand life enough to complain about it, it's too late. Your psyche is already "baked."

If you ended up in a mean and nasty situation, that does seem cruel, but you still have opportunity. You can create positive intersubjective interactions anyway. In that way you develop your intersubjective intuition over time and upgrade the patterns of your Planck Code.

People are born every day into poverty, cruelty, slavery, disease and suffering. Those are not personal shortcomings of any kind. One's physical and social circumstances are consequences of intra-psychic and sub-personal forces beyond a person's control.

Conversely, being born into privilege is not any kind of virtue. Virtue and deficiency arise from the quality of intersubjective interactions one engages in, not from the objective quality of one's circumstances.

In the large scheme of experience, which is only known in outline from the pseudo-omniscience of a MPM point of view, it's difficult to assess the meaning of any one period of experience. We ordinary Garden-dwellers can only focus on the quality of immediate intersubjective interaction. We have no direct mental access to our Planck Code because it's inside the BHN where there is no mentality.

Everybody's got a different Planck Code so it doesn't make much sense to complain that someone else's situation is better than yours. It's not the objective situation that matters. Experience is all about intersubjective intentionality and accommodation. You can't tell by casually looking at someone what's going on with them.

It is also worth noting that since BHNs are extremely frequent in the course of experience, your Big Con is rebuilt innumerable times each day. There is no lack of opportunity for change.

Socialization vs Reindeering

In the beginning, the new SRS issues intentional acts to rid itself of residual Commodity Subjectivity. In so doing, it projects self-objects that congeal into an objectified otherness that is fundamentally intersubjective in nature. The intersubjective others in turn provide scaffolding for further learning that leads to ever-more-intentionally-focused objects. That is the Reindeer process.

Socialization is not the same as Reindeering. Socialization mainly engages the bodily SMC and intellectual SLM modules of mind. Reindeering is pre-cognitive and pre-personal. Reindeering sets the stage for socialization.

We can study socialization in detail, and have done so, as the rich literature of developmental psychology attests. But that study begins rather late in the process. Reindeering begins with individuation and continues through establishment, in the Outer Fold, of the parameters defining how socialization will occur.

Reincarnation Reconsidered

The quality of early Reindeer processes affects the quality of later socialization, which in turn is critical in constitution of the

Big Con for each individual, including the establishment of the physical body.

Considering the long chain of processes that make up the Recon leading to Big Con reality, we see that questions of embodiment only arise much further down the line. Reincarnation, even if the doctrine were plausible, does not address the most important parts of the Reconstruction process. We need to examine the Reconstruction of embodiment with fresh eyes.

The Bod Con

As the Reconstruction (Recon) proceeds in the Outward Fold, one of the most important tasks is establishment of an individual sense of embodiment. I designate that sub-process separately as the Bod Con (short for Body Construction).

Like all of the reconstructed world, one's body is a reification of subjective intentional projections. Self-objects solidify into free-standing objective reality with the amnesia of reification. By the time that bodily objectivity is subsequently accommodated, it presents itself as free-standing, "external," mind-independent, and self-existent. That's true of all objects, including one's own body.

The Bod Con happens long before the development of the mature, three-part mind that includes cognitive processes such as "making things up." So it's not true that we mentally "make up" body and world. No individual alone even has the resources to project a body. The BodCon is done collaboratively with the individual's social community through the long, tedious process of socialization.

Steps of the Bod Con

We can make a crude timeline of how the process goes (remembering that time is elastic in the Outward Fold):

1. BHN. Within the BHN, there is no body, no self, no world.

2. Individuation. A bubble of subjectivity of the individual self-relating kind (SRS) forms in the field of impersonal Commodity subjectivity. When that SRS node acts, a quantum of

mentality arises, and we can say "an individual" is born (without a body or a world).

3. The Social Other. The first objects to appear to the new SRS are social others. The SRS is always proto-aware of a surrounding self-alien otherness. In particular, one big social object, the mother or other primary caregiver is discerned. "Mother" at this point, is a dimly apprehended blob of not-self "other." (There is still no body, from the first-person point of view).

4. Implied Embodiment. Mother gives you your body, as detailed in *Mind Without Body* (Adams, 2021b). The sense of having a body forms gradually over the course of interaction with the otherness later known as mother.

At first, everything is just a "blooming, buzzing confusion" (to use William James's famous phrase). For the individual, it is not even clear what is "me" and what is not. But gradually, distinctions are made. For example, mother goes away sometimes, but "I" remain. Therefore, mother must be something different from me.

Over time, mother points out your body parts. These are your toes, look! Wiggly-wiggly! The infant tacitly correlates perception, proprioception, and motor output. With repetition, that sort of interaction creates toes in the infant's experience. Later, mother goes away but the toes do not. That means these are *my* toes. And voila, your mother has given you toes.

In a similar way, one's body, inside and out, sensory and motor, comes into first-person experience through social interaction. It's a very long process. You are born without a body. Your body has to be given to you by the community. (I'm glossing past intra-uterine interaction between mother and child for the sake of explanatory simplicity).

Of course, Mother has no clue that she is giving the infant a body. From her point of view, the body already exists. In her mind, all she's doing is interacting with the infant. What she believes about bodies is what her contextual community believes. Through her, the community communicates to the newborn what the beliefs and expectations are in that culture for a human body.

Note that Mom does not say "Look! Here are your metatarsals and ligaments! And here is your mitochondrial RNA!" Mom does not know that level of body detail and has no need to. Toes are important; everybody knows that. She gives toes.

The rest of it, the internals, the details—that is not common knowledge in the socialization community and is not transmitted during primary socialization. It is translated much, much later, by the intellectual socialization community of schoolteachers, physicians and biologists, and textbooks and even then only to those who might be interested.

5. Body Schema and World. Over time, the infant develops a sense of an embodied self through correlations of sensory input and motor output. Again, all of it is tacit understanding, not cognitive.

A "body schema" sounds intellectual, but it's not. It's a term borrowed from Merleau-Ponty (1946). The body is not a shell we drag around with us, but the medium or "schema" through which the mind lives its life.

With the Body Schema, the individual is able to construct the world with help from the rapidly growing socialization community. It seems impossible to us now that every detail of the world was painstakingly learned, but in fact, every single person does it that way. We call it "learning" the world because we're in it now, but from the new individual's perspective, it's a long process of mental *construction*, not passive absorption of what already was there.

6. Medical Body and Self. With completion of the tripartite mind that comes with language acquisition, one learns to explicitly conceptualize the body, its functions and actions, its capacities and limitations. The "external" world becomes reified into permanent otherness, as does the social community. Foggy otherness becomes discriminated into "other people," and "things out there."

One refines a synthetic idea of the generalized human body based on the collective wisdom of the community, as presented for example in biology books. The individual comes to believe in the physical body as an objective, physical otherness, an object no different in principle than other objects in the physical world. That's when you get metatarsals in your feet, not before.

Much confusion about one's own body—why it does what it does, why it doesn't do what we'd like it to do—comes from not understanding the structure of the tripartite mind. The SLM crudely conceptualizes and reifies "embodied" experience like feelings, pains, and intuitions into a physical "body." That locates proprioception in space and time, and connects it to the SLM's sense of agency and ipseity. Nevertheless, the reified body remains as not quite compatible with the mind. The medical textbook confirms that. It does not contain a mind, only a physical brain.

Along with conceptualization of the medical body, one develops a sense of selfhood based on interactions with others. One learns "what other people think." That social self becomes reified and is also conceptually "located" inside the medical body. It's a short step then to the paradoxical mind-body problem: *How* could a mind be *located* in a body?

The mind-body problem (aka mind-brain problem) is a nonsensical riddle atop a pile of false assumptions about body, self, and world, but it's a perfectly understandable consequence of the process of the BodCon during the Recon.

Biology

The physical body, described as the "medical body" is an object conceptualized from the third-person point of view. It is a thoroughly reified mental object we maintain intellectually alongside the tacit first-person body, the body schema.

Since our culture privileges the third-person point of view, we are convinced that our biological body is a certain configuration of meat, bones, and neurons, no different in principle from the constituents of a chimpanzee, a fish, or banana. We fail to realize that such a view of the body is an unwitting conflation of first-person experience with third-person conceptualization.

Part of the definition of the medical body is that it has no mentality. It's just a biological machine reducible to physics and chemistry. But the mind is 100% mental and 0% physical. Blending those unblendable ideas gives us the confused idea of embodiment: a mentality surrounded by a non-mental body. We accept that as the fact of experience, even though it makes no sense and even though our actual mental experience is nothing like that.

Sex

From an adult's point of view, a baby is "born" when it emerges from the womb. Before that, it was living inside the womb. It grew there from an embryo, and before that, from a blastula, and before that, it arose from merged zygotes, a merger from interaction between the parents.

Having sex is a conversation in the medium of bodies. That particular kind of conversation is nonverbal but deeply intersubjective. Having sex is not like accidentally bumping into someone on a crowded street. It's an intentional act of intersubjectivity. The intentionality may be conceptualized in many ways by the participants, but one component is that it can produce a third person, a baby.

One tacit aim of sexual intercourse is always to individuate a new consciousness separate from either parent, and yet still also part of both parents. One implicit meaning of the sex act is to jointly produce an intersubjective other through the physical process of individuation.

That goal is usually not conscious. We have all kinds of conscious and even subconscious reasons for having sex. Those can include recreation, social intimacy, commerce, family planning, and many others. Nevertheless the dance of the bodies remains a third-person account of the beginning of corporeal individuation. Sex is an intersubjective conversation that begins long before the physical encounter of the bodies. It begins in language and other social behavior.

In my description of the Bod Con, a sub-process embedded in the larger Recon process, embodiment occurs quite far down the line of individuation events. But it does occur, and the objective, biological account of reproduction is not wrong. Biology is simply a story that doesn't start at the beginning.

Continuity of the Body

If the body is reconstructed after every BHN, why does it seem like we have the same body over time? Each morning, we wake up to a new day, but the body feels like the same one we went to bed with. Why would that be so if it's a total rebuild? Let's zoom in on that next.

Memory

Mind, body, world, and community are all constructed afresh after each BHN. Yet experience seems continuous before and after. More often than not, the BHN itself is not even noticed as life continues smoothly.

That smooth continuation can be seen as illusory when considered from a special point of view. The Marco Polo traveler, who has a imagined omniscient point of view, can understand post-BHN experience as "new construction." In the ordinary, first-person point of view, there is no Reconstruction. We don't want to confuse those two points of view. You can't hold the MPM and the ordinary view at once. You can only oscillate between them.

Taking just the theoretical, pseudo-omniscient perspective of the MPM traveler, what *is* the explanation of the apparent continuity of experience over BHNs? If a BHN wipes out everything, why *is* today continuous with yesterday?

Self-Recognition is not Memory

When you look in a mirror, you don't *remember* yourself from past images and say, *yes, that's me, all right. I remember that image from yesterday.* The experience is not like picking out your face from a set of police mug shots. Rather, you non-cognitively accommodate the objective image in the glass to your expectations. The recognition is without mnemonic coloration.

A similar phenomenology prevails during the accommodation phase of each mental act, when SRS confronts and (proto-) recognizes objects. SRS metaphorically says, "Hey, that's me!" It recognizes itself in the object, which is how "recognizing" an object is accomplished.

Those terms of recognizing an object are,

"That's" = the object.

"Me" = the subject, SRS.

"Hey" = the conversion self-alien objectivity into familiar subjectivity.

Accommodation melts the alien quality of an object and puts up a shiny original as a mirror to SRS. Object recognition is really subjective self-recognition. The River of Forgetfulness is bridged when SRS metaphorically recognizes itself in the object.

In psychology textbooks, *recognition* is classified as one of the many kinds of memory but that's misleading. So-called "recognition memory" in psychology really describes prompted recall. You are presented with a list of terms, or a set of cards or objects, and asked to pick the ones you've seen before. In other words, which ones do you "recognize?"

But unlike the dynamics of recognition in the QMP cycle, that kind of "recognition" involves comparing each object with recalled memories of similar objects. It amounts to selective recall. The test subject says, "I recognize this one because I recall seeing it before."

QMP recognition does not work like that. It involves no explicit recall. It's an immediate self-awareness through object-recognition. That's why I say SRS self-recognition is called accommodation, not a kind of recall as memory is traditionally described.

Accommodation Creates Memory

SRS (metaphorically) reconfigures itself to include the object within its subjective domain. The object is then no longer "out there," but "in here." It has become part of "me." SRS has "expanded" itself and repatriated the object. That defines satisfaction of the intentional act that projected the object in the first place.

At accommodation, the former object does not disappear. It is "gone" as a self-alien object, but persists as a qualitative region within the domain of SRS ipseity, or sense of self. That's because SRS becomes slightly different after each BHN. It is no longer identical with the pre-BHN SRS because it now "contains" the subjective analog of the recently accommodated object.

Extended to the context of death as a BHN, we can say that the Reconstruction will never produce a new individual, community, and world identical to the pre-death one (from the MPM point of view). Every life is different because each new individuation of subjectivity is moderated by an updated Planck Code.

The texture of the post-BHN SRS can bias it to project self-objects previously accommodated. That's how we manage to drill away at a single problem over time and over innumerable mental cycles. If that were not so, accommodated objects would go out of existence. You'd recognize something and it would disappear. You couldn't have two thoughts about one object.

Instead, a similar cluster of objects keeps getting re-absorbed and reprojected with minor variations in both the objects and the SRS occurring on each cycle. Post-BHN experience is "familiar" in a construed autobiographical history not because of memory, but because the accommodation process is affected by its own success in finding teleological satisfaction.

Non-Homuncular Memory

In one reading of the above account, the SRS acts as the homunculus in a storage-and-retrieval model of memory in that it readily "recognizes" self-objects. That is an unsubtle reading, however. There are several reasons why mental accommodation is not like a storage-and-retrieval memory.

1. SRS is not a mind and cannot act mentally. Mental acts require all the elements of a complete QMP cycle. By definition, SRS cannot act as a homunculus.

2. The SRS "expansion" that annexes the object is not an intentional act. Rather, it is an accommodative act, much as a dry sponge expands to absorb water. The absence of intentionality rules out homuncular memory-action by SRS.

3. The object never gets stored. Rather, features of the *relationship* between subject and object are logged into the Planck Code. A similar object can be reconstructed from Planck Code traces, but the original object was never stored. Again, an object storage-and-retrieval interpretation is ruled out.

4. The Planck Code "resides" in the BHN where there is no time. The SRS is in time, as is the QMP cycle. The accommodation is therefore timeless. Any description of "storage" in the absence of time is contradictory.

5. The seeming "transfer" of features of the subject-object relationship from SRS to Planck Code is an illusion of point of view. The SRS ceases to exist at onset of the BHN, and with it, mentality and the first-person point of view. Only the fictional MPM traveler can talk about indexing motivational satisfaction to the Planck Code.

Conclusion

The world is recreated anew after each BHN, in the first-person point of view, yet from that point of view, the world also seems continuous across multiple BHNs. What accounts for that paradox?

In part, it's a simple point of view confusion. In each person's point of view, the world is not a recreation. It is the only world the person has ever known. BHNs, if they are recognized at all, are merely anomalous blips in continuous autobiographical memory.

The "paradox" of seeming continuity across BHNs is only a paradox for a person who assumes the point of view of a Marco Polo traveler. To the MPM traveler, the BHN is a Destroyer of Worlds. A complete reconstruction of self and world is required afterward. But even then, there is no paradox, for the MPM traveler understands each Reconstruction for what it is, unburdened by questions of continuity. The paradox arises only when we confuse those two points of view. Failing to discriminate the two points of view results in the seeming paradox.

Memory is a poor explanation of the apparent continuity, for if a BHN dissolves body, mind, and world, nothing remains to support memory across the gap. I have proposed that reconstruction of the body, the Bod Con, is an alternative to a memory explanation of the seeming continuity. The elements of mentality that survive a BHN are sufficient for reconstruction of a body that can be accepted as familiar.

The difference between the kind of non-homuncular reconstruction of the Bod Con and traditional definitions of memory may not be perfectly crisp. However, the Recon and particularly the Bod Con provide better accounts of traditional memory than memory can provide for our sense of a continuous autobiography.

Holding in mind the fact that the Ordinary and the MPM points of view are oscillatory and not simultaneous, perhaps we can accept both accounts, each in its own context. Generalizing that mental gymnastic leads to an interesting reconceptualization of the geometry of death and life.

The Great Necker Cube

Some people think of death as a new beginning, part of an ongoing larger cycle of life and death. We love the caterpillar-to-butterfly story. Casting death as a recurrent and self-terminating BHN encourages such a view.

The present analysis does not, however, suggest a grand cycle of life and death as many traditional accounts of reincarnation do. Instead, it proposes ongoing oscillation between alternate realities in living, experiential time. Important differences are implied by those two images.

1. The Great Wheel

In Hinduism, the cycle of death and rebirth through reincarnation forms a Great Wheel. By getting off the wheel, you no longer endure the suffering of earthly existence. You supposedly get off the wheel (according to some versions) by abandoning all personal desires and accepting that your soul is the same as God.

Buddhists say by freeing ourselves from desire, we escape the relentless accumulation of karma and achieve nirvana, which is tantamount to getting off the wheel.

The Great Wheel is a conceptualization that visualizes life, death, and rebirth from a point of view outside all that. But what is that point of view? Where would you be if you got off the wheel? And why would that be an unalloyed good? You'd be neither alive nor dead. You'd be nothing. Is nothing good?

The "wheel" metaphor suggests cycles without end. It assumes one should get off that ride. But even if I wanted to, when would I do it? Now? After I'm dead?

And how would I get off? Would the music stop, and I would head to the exit gate? Exiting to what? The wheel metaphor presupposes an impossible God's-eye view, a point of view I don't have. I'm pretty sure no human has it. I propose an alternative geometry.

2. The Great Necker Cube

The Necker Cube is an illustration invented by Luis Necker in 1832. Assuming the cube-drawing represents an object in the world, the viewer's imagined bodily orientation to it is ambiguous.

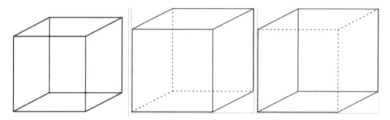

Figure 6. Necker Cube (left) with alternate viewing orientations.

What's interesting about the Necker Cube in this context is that one generally cannot see both orientations at once. You can see one or the other. What happens between the two orientations? Literally, nothing. There seems to be no transition. I think that's a better metaphor for the relation between life and death than the Great Wheel.

Unlike with the Great Wheel, one can maintain one's grounded, human, realistic point of view of the Necker Cube because it isn't transcendental. It's just a shift in mental perspective. You can experience it anytime. You don't need to "get off" the Great Necker Cube.

The Necker Cube oscillates virtual points of view. Why does the mental machinery switch between one orientation and the other? A simple explanation is that visual neurology attempts to reconcile its information with the brain's motor system. As we have almost no introspective access to our brain, we can't track anything during those interactions. From a first-person, experiential point of view therefore, there is no transition.

But that cannot be the whole story because considerable self-reflective, conceptualized experience is also required to support interest in the Necker Cube. I doubt that any non-human animal would find the illustration interesting. A lot of mentality is embedded in the illusion.

Metaphorically, we can say that the two orientations of the Necker Cube mark the transition between the Garden of ordinary experience defined by the Big Con and a Black Hole of Nothingness (BHN). We can imaginatively explore each orientation, but not both. The transition between them remains opaque, a non-experience, a mini-BHN.

Philosopher Gottfried Leibniz flourished around 1700, well before the Necker Cube was invented. His world had only one point of view from which he famously asked, "Why is there something rather than nothing?" It's an odd question, one that doesn't come up if you're totally immersed in the Big Con. It's only when you stick your head above the Garden wall that you wonder. Leibniz stuck his head out, saw nothingness, and was confused. His final answer to the question was "God deems it so."

Martin Heidegger, taking up Leibniz's question two and a half centuries later, had a different answer. He said "There is no such thing as nothing." Reality is entirely something. Heidegger was not a head-sticker-outer. If we were utterly incapable of escaping the Big Con, Heidegger would be right. But first-person analysis of subjectivity (not Heidegger's forte), gives us access to BHN nothingness all around us.

My answer to Leibniz is: There is something *and* there is nothing. They oscillate like a Necker Cube. We can see both realities, but not at the same time. It's a very unstable experience. We prefer not to look. We prefer to stay immersed in the Big Con where reality makes more sense.

As to the thrust of Leibniz's question: "Why?" I don't know. That's the way I found it.

Necker Cube Analysis

The Great Necker Cube is a real-time oscillation of subjective points of view on a single object. The points of view involve different implied locations of one's body in space and time. Of the two alternative orientations shown to the right in *Figure 6*, if you were going to reach out and pick up the one in the middle,

A. you would be located about straight-ahead from the middle of the cube but slightly above it. You would reach forward and slightly down to get it.

For the cube on the rightmost side of the drawing, the implied "you" is located either

B. To the right of the cube and slightly above. The cube is below. You would reach down and left to pick it up.

C. Below and to the left of the cube. The cube is above your line of vision. Grabbing it would require you to reach up and to the right. This is the most awkward position to get a feel for. You have to take the solid-line rhombus at the bottom of the illustration as the bottom of the cube seen from below.

For all three subjective orientations to the cube, you don't do anything so physical as actual reaching and grabbing. You sit in your chair and imagine yourself in different locations in "picture space," the imaginary space implied by the cube (as if it were a real cube).

Let's call the imagined subjective *you* in picture space a *proprius*, just to give it a name. You have three propriuses in this demonstration. They are described above. Each proprius is imaginarily embodied, located in imaginary time and space. If subjectivity were not always embodied, the illusion wouldn't work. Your point of view is an embodied proprius in picture-space.

The transitions between propriuses seem to be instantaneous, even though you can "nudge" one proprius to the fore over the others with certain eye movements on certain parts of the drawing.

That foregoing analysis of the Necker Cube illusion shows how the transition among alternate propriuses maps to the transitions between ordinary experience and the imaginary experience of the MPM point of view, and back again. It's a lateral move in space, not a circular move in time like the Great Wheel.

The reason the Necker cube geometry is a better descriptor is that subjectivity is always embodied and always located somewhere in space. Time comes and goes, stretches and contracts. It may be altogether illusory. But space is unquestionable for an embodied mind.

Fractal Death

Death In Mind is an exploration that begins from a simple idea: What if death is a BHN like all the others? To explore this idea, we defined death as a first-person phenomenon, a condition of consciousness—in fact, the cessation of it. The physical, biological aspect of death was a minor consideration.

Perhaps the most startling consequence of taking death as a BHN is that it terminates. Though nobody has reported credible post-death experience, our knowledge of other BHNs predicts that death eventually would end and some kind of self-aware consciousness would emerge, though not the "same" consciousness as before.

Assuming death does terminate, what comes after? Again by comparison to ordinary BHNs, we can say what should happen. There would be an Outward Fold, as there is for other BHNs, during which self-relating subjectivity establishes a first-person point of view. That point of view goes on to define a world outside itself.

The changes within and after a BHN suggest parallels with traditional accounts of death and reincarnation. While reincarnation is not coherent, plausible, or necessary in the current context, consciousness as we know it is always embodied. Close examination of the post-BHN Outward Fold suggests how a physical body and the entire physical world might be reconstructed "from scratch" after every BHN.

The Fractal View

I have labeled this new view of death the *Fractal View* to distinguish it from others. Here's how it compares to other accounts.

Popular View

Death is not really final. You just "pass on" to a special place beyond Earth, somehow living again, but in happiness, your mind and body somehow intact. You are no longer in time, but immortal, even though time is necessary for change, and if nothing changes life is inconceivable.

Cyclical View

Death is the end of your time on Earth but not the absolute end. After 49 days, according to *The Tibetan Book of the Dead*, time starts up again for you in a new body. However, when you rejoin the living, you don't remember anything, recognize anything, nor does anyone recognize you. Repeat endlessly.

Standard View

Death is personal oblivion at the end of a life. There's no epilogue, no recovery, no do-over. The rest of the world continues as before but you're "out" for good.

Fractal View

BHNs punctuate all of experience. Death is just another BHN.

Fractal Imagery

A fractal is a mathematical idea involving a recursive function. In fractal imagery, the function produces an image that repeats in ever-smaller-scale forever.

In the Fractal View of death, the smallest BHNs might be compared to microscopic particles. BHNs like dreamless sleep could be imagined as spheres ranging from the size of tennis balls to beach balls. Death, the big one, is like a view of the moon from five miles out. It's so big you can't even see around it. But they're all identical BHNs in structure and function, differing only in scale.

Keeping with the imagery of multi-sized BHNs, how are they organized? In fractal each part has all the properties of the whole. A famous fractal image example is the Apollonian Gasket.

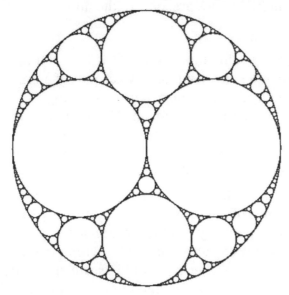

Figure 7 Apollonian Gasket

The fractal approach seems a fair representation of BHNs. Yet the idea of "smaller" and "larger" BHNs is difficult because BHNs themselves are not spatial. Each BHN is not an area but a separate blip in experience.

Time Fractals as an Organizing Principle

A "blip" is an event in time. To be a blip, some time must pass, otherwise, there could be no events. If we think of BHNs as longer or shorter periods of time, we still want to ask how they are organized with respect to each other.

Fractals of time are possible, They're difficult to imagine, but mathematically well-defined. If we take each circle in the Apollonian Gasket to represent a duration in time, we get the idea that "larger" BHNs take more time than "smaller" ones, which is how we describe them in ordinary experience.

Figure 7 suggests that BHNs of all durations are "contained within" the largest one. They are not lined up sequentially as a string of events in ordinary linear time. Does that mean they all proceed at once? That doesn't make much sense for ordinary experience but perhaps we can say, from an imaginary MPM point of view, that all BHNs "are present" in the now.

Memory Vs Oscillation

An interesting and useful implication of the fractal time view of BHNs is that it obviates the need for any account of memory. If everything is happening now, memory has no meaning. If ordinary experience is "actually" (from an MPM point of view) just the zones between the circles of the Apollonian Gasket, then we can say that our traditional concept of memory is a story we use to "straighten out" fractal time to match cultural ideas.

Fractal time is a difficult idea to conceptualize but there is some scientific evidence of micro-biological rhythmicity in a fractal pattern (Bandyopadhyay (2020)). Neural activity in a network sometimes shows a pattern of triples within triples, just as fractal time would suggest. Perhaps could use an alternative conceptual context to reframe our understanding of biological activity and temporal experience.

In the multiverse theory derived from quantum physics, simultaneous parallel universes of space, time and causality continue independently. Ordinary experience only knows the world it lives in, yet from an omniscient point of view, alternatives are simultaneously present. That idea is consistent with the notion of oscillatory dualism presented in this essay. You only know the reality that you know, but another (within the BHN) is accessible at almost any time. In the oscillatory model, the multiple realities are not simultaneous but alternating.

The Fractal View of death, along with the notion of the Great Necker Cube, suggests that it is possible to oscillate from the familiar default into another reality and back again. These paradoxical thoughts remind us that ordinary experience is perforated by entities (BHNs) that do not conform to ordinary notions of time and space, but which are revealed by the MPM point of view.

Fractal Death

With this fractal view of death, we can say that death and reconstruction occur repeatedly, identically, but on different time scales. That is consistent with the evidence from examining BHNs as we have done in this essay.

In the fractal view, death is not a singularity at the end of life. It's a prolonged version of an ordinary BHN. Considering the smaller BHNs as fractal instances, we can say each of us has already died and reconstructed life many times, and will continue to do so. Death is thus an everyday event, ubiquitous in human experience.

As an ordinary person living under the spell of the Big Con like everybody else, I have trouble making sense of events outside the linear sequence of traditional autobiographical experience. A fractal view, where everything is "all at once" is beyond my ability to intuit. Even so, I recognize it as a logical possibility.

Advantages of Considering Death as a BHN

What does this view of death as a "big" fractal BHN offer that other views do not? It has at least these virtues.

1. A Principled Account

Looking at death as an ordinary BHN is a conceptualization based on observation and reason, unlike other accounts based on faith, hope, authority, tradition or fantasy. We can observe ordinary BHNs in detail using appropriate techniques, and we can compare those observations to what we know and infer about death. If we find the comparisons convincing, we can reasonably reconceptualize death. That gives us a first-person, psychological description of death with credentials of fact and reason.

2. Not Nothing

Death ordinarily confronts us with the blank stare of emptiness. The prospect of absolute erasure is not even the worst of it. Confronting the End of Everything also renders all prior experience retroactively meaningless. We find no pot of gold at the end, no reward for a life well-lived. There's only the abyss. Nothing could be more bleak.

There's no evidence or reason to hope that one's body or mind survive death. Yet we conclude that something does persist because self-relating consciousness with a first-person point of view emerges in the Outward Fold of all other BHNs. That's not nothing.

One's Planck Code persists across every BHN. But the first-person point of view perishes. Therefore, a person does have some influence now over what goes into the Planck Code now, even though no person survives the BHN to experience the effects of its readout. Still, it's good to know that every encounter, every intentional act, has an effect on the future Recon. That's not nothing.

3. The Future

Another advantage that falls out of this investigation is that there *is* a future. If my death is just a big BHN, it will terminate, and when it does, some kind of SRS-based consciousness will emerge, and there *will* be a future, even though it won't include me.

The Big Con is not a reality into which we are helplessly thrown. It's a construction, a spun web built in collaboration with a social community. It's designed to meet everyone's collective psychological needs. We have woven that web before. It will be woven again. The absolute "end of everything" is not a prospect.

4. The Community

We have deduced from observational evidence that Commodity Subjectivity survives BHNs. That is the nonindividuated "substance" from which individuals form. The possibility of intersubjective consciousness made up of self-aware individuals therefore survives death. We need not worry about all conscious communities "going extinct." Death cannot obliterate the possibility of intersubjective communities.

5. Motivating Force

The Motivating Force that drives individuation out of Commodity Subjectivity survives BHNs. Therefore, there will always be individuating (proto-)self-aware subjectivities (SRS) bubbling up. "The world" cannot end in an absolute way because of that. Furthermore, since individuals retain tacit awareness of Commodity Subjectivity and forever struggle try to eject it, we can say there will always be creativity. Death does not negate the essence of creativity.

Disadvantages of the Fractal View

The Fractal View of Death as a "big" BHN does have some problems. Chief among them is plausibility. Because the Big Con and especially the Bod Con are so compelling, it's easy to prefer the standard third-person account of BHNs: the brain changes in such a way that consciousness goes "off." When the brain resumes, as upon awakening, consciousness comes back on. In death, the brain never comes back on, and that defines the end of consciousness.

It's a compelling story. The problem is that there is no conceivable interface between brains and minds from a third-person point of view. Minds cannot be observed in that point of view, only brains. There is no strictly third-person evidence for the existence of minds. Even the alleged correlation between brains and minds depends on undocumented, promiscuous shifting to a subjective point of view.

Since BHNs are mental phenomena, a story about brain activity cannot legitimately make contact with the phenomenon of interest. Mental phenomena are simply not susceptible to the methods of science, which measures only objectivity and not subjectivity. It follows that no scientific account of reality can, in principle, ever be complete (under current understanding of science).

Despite that obvious and airtight reasoning, the zeitgeist scientific account of reality is extremely hard to resist. Conversely, the first-person account of BHN-death and the Big Con is a difficult alternative to take seriously.

Another drawback to the Fractal View is the difficulty in maintaining the point of view it requires.

The default view of death is objective. We typically conceptualize not our own but someone else's death, perhaps someone we knew. They were here, they died, they didn't come back. Now they're physically and intersubjectively gone. The third-person, objective point of view makes it look like death is a permanent terminus of life. It does not suggest that death is a recurring fractal pattern in experience.

To appreciate the Fractal View of death, one must instead take the fictional Marco-Polo point of view from Otherland, the fictive interior of a BHN. Time near the border of Otherland is elastic. The difference between the survivors at a funeral and the deceased is just a few ticks of a rubber clock.

The funeral-goers are shoring up their Big Con at the funeral. That's what it's for. A funeral is a collaborative social reinforcement of the default story of death.

But meanwhile, across the street from the funeral, at a hospital, a baby is born and an individuated and embodied subjectivity begins the long task of collaboratively constructing a world to live in. The community celebrates the biological birth in ceremonies and festivities that shore up the collaborative story of birth.

A newborn is immortal. Animals (and infants and children) that don't conceptualize their own mental processes don't know anything about death. It is not even a remote prospect for them. They are indeed functionally immortal from a first-person point of view.

Conclusion

The Recon leads to a world derived from the three seeds that persist over a BHN. Those seeds derive from lived experience. It's a self-reinforcing loop that's extremely hard to deviate from.

Within the loop, we see ourselves as biological beings with a dash of intersubjective connection. From that objective point of view, we are very much mortal.

But why privilege the third-person, object-oriented, biological self-definition over the first-person point of view? Because that's how life in the Garden goes, at least in the region where I live, at this moment in history. In the Garden, reality is objective and the wall is an unquestioned boundary. At least that's true for those who have never been outside and suspect nothing.

This thesis suggests there's another landscape beyond the wall.

References

Adams, William (2005). What Does it All Mean? A Humanistic Account of Human Experience. Exeter, U.K.: Imprint Academic.

Adams, William X. (2020). *Scientific Introspection: Tools to Reveal the Mind*. https://www.psifibooks.com/books-from-psifibooks-com/

Adams, William X. (2021a). *Mind Without Brain: A Proposal*. https://www.psifibooks.com/books-from-psifibooks-com/

Adams, William X. (2021b). *Mind, Body, World*. https://www.psifibooks.com/books-from-psifibooks-com/

Adams, William X. (2023a). *Nothing in Mind*. https://www.psifibooks.com/books-from-psifibooks-com/

Adams, William X. (2023b). *Polters*. https://www.psifibooks.com/books-from-psifibooks-com/

Author (2021). The physical process of dying. *Australia: Health Direct*. Online at
https://www.healthdirect.gov.au/the-physical-process-of-dying

Ball, Philip (2018). *Beyond Weird*. Chicago: University of Chicago Press.

Bandyopadhyay, Anirban (2020). Nanobrain: *The Making of an Artificial Brain from a Time Crystal*. Boca Raton, Fl.: CRC Press /Taylor & Francis, 354 pp.

Bergson, Henri (1889). *Time and Free Will*. New York: Dover. Available online at https://www.gutenberg.org/files/56852/56852-h/56852-h.htm

Bible, the King James Version (2017). Peabody, MA: Christian Art Publishers.

Botticelli, Sandro (ca. 1485) *The Birth of Venus.* https://en.wikipedia.org/wiki/The_Birth_of_Venus.

Buber, Martin (1937/1970). *I and Thou.* New York: Simon & Schuster-Touchstone.

Butler, J. (1990). Gender Trouble: Feminism and the Subversion of Identity. NY: Routledge.

Butzer, B. (2021). Does Synchronicity Point Us Towards the Fundamental Nature of Consciousness? *Journal of Consciousness Studies*, 28, (3-4), pp. 29-54.

Calvino, Italo (1972). *Invisible Cities.* New York: Harvest/HBJ.

Cambridge University Press & Assessment (2023). *Reincarnation.* Cambridge, U.K. Retrieved July 2023 from https://dictionary.cambridge.org/us/dictionary/english/reincarnation.

Campuzano, Juan Carlos Ponce (2018). *Strange Attractors: Interactive 3D Simulations of Dynamic Mathematics.* Online at https://www.dynamicmath.xyz/strange-attractors

Carskadon M, & Dement W. (2005). Normal human sleep: An overview. In: Kryger, M.H., Roth, T., and Dement, W.C., (Eds). *Principles and Practice of Sleep Medicine.* 4th ed. Philadelphia: Elsevier Saunders, pp. 13–23.

Carskadon, M.A., & Dement, W.C. (2011). Monitoring and staging human sleep. In M.H. Kryger, T. Roth, & W.C. Dement (Eds.), P*rinciples and practice of sleep medicine, 5th edition*, (pp 16-26). St. Louis: Elsevier Saunders.

Combes, Muriel (2013). Gilbert Simondon and the Philosophy of the Transindividual. Cambridge, MA: The MIT Press.

Dear, Jennie (2016). *What It Feels Like to Die. The Atlantic*, September 9, 2016.

Dorje, Gyurme (Trans.) (2005). *The Tibetan Book of the Dead*. New York: Penguin.

Fiske, Donald. W. (1949). Consistency of the factorial structures of personality ratings from different sources. *The Journal of Abnormal and Social Psychology*, 44 (3), 329-344. doi.org/10.1037/h0057198

Gibson, J. J. (1966). *The Senses Considered as Perceptual Systems*. Boston, MA: Houghton Mifflin.

Gödel Kurt (1931). On formally undecidable theorems of Principia Mathematica and related systems *I*. *Monthly Magazines for Mathematics and Physics* 38(1),173–198.

Grosz, Elizabeth (2017). The Incorporeal: Ontology, Ethics, and the Limits of Materialism. New York: Columbia University Press.

Hathaway, S. R., & McKinley, J. C. (1943). *The Minnesota Multiphasic Personality Inventory (Rev. ed., 2nd printing)*. University of Minnesota Press.

Herbert, Nick (1985). *Quantum Reality*. New York: Anchor.

Letheby, Chris (2021). *Philosophy of Psychedelics*. Oxford: Oxford University Press.

Merleau-Ponty Maurice (2012/1945). Phenomenology of Perception. Trans. Donald A. Landes. New York: Routledge. (Phénoménologie de la perception. Paris: Gallimard, 1945.)

Metzner, R., Alpert, R., and T. Leary (1964). The Psychedelic Experience: A Manual Based on The Tibetan Book of the Dead, as cited by Greenfield, Robert (2006). *Timothy Leary: A Biography*. Harcourt Publishers.

National Heart, Lung, and Blood Institute (NHLBI). (2022). *Sleep Deprivation and Deficiency: How Sleep Affects Your Health*. Retrieved June 9, 2023. https://www.nhlbi.nih.gov/health/sleep-deprivation/health-effects

Noe, Alva (2006) *Action in Perception*. The MIT Press.

Rovelli, Carlo (2014). *Reality is Not What it Seems*. New York: Riverhead Books.

Simondon, Gilbert (2020). *Individuation in Light of Notions of Form and Information*. Minneapolis: University of Minnesota Press.

Smart, J.J.C. (1959). Sensations and Brain Processes. *Philosophical Review*, 68 (April):141-56.

Tamaki, M., Wang, Z., Barnes-Diana, T.et al.(2020). Complementary contributions of non-REM and REM sleep to visual learning. *Nature Neuroscience* 23, 1150–1156. https://doi.org/10.1038/s41593-020-0666-y

Van Gordon, William; Shonin, Edo; Dunn, Thomas J.; Sapthiang, Supakyada; Kotera, Yasuhiro; Garcia-Campayo, Javier; & Sheffield, David (2019). Exploring Emptiness and its Effects on Non-attachment, Mystical Experiences, and Psycho-spiritual Wellbeing: A Quantitative and Qualitative Study of Advanced Meditators. *Explore* Vol. 15 (4), July–August, pp. 261-272.

Van Heijenoort, J. (ed.) (1967). *From Frege to Gödel: A Source Book in Mathematical Logic, 1879–1931*. Cambridge, MA: Harvard University Press.

Vogel GW. A review of REM sleep deprivation. *Archives of General Psychiatry*. 1975 Jun;32(6):749-61. doi: 10.1001/archpsyc.1975.01760240077006. PMID: 165795.

Want More?

NONFICTION PHILOSOPHICAL PSYCHOLOGY

See www.psifibooks.com for titles by William X. Adams that you can purchase at your favorite retailer. Here's where to get the links you need:

https://www.psifibooks.com/books-from-psifibooks-com/

Discovering the Mind Series

This series of monographs is the result of a fifty-year hunt for the mind. What is it? How does it work? Eventually, the main question became, "Who's asking?"

The first book in the series, *Scientific Introspection*, wrestles with method. As far as we can tell, we humans are the only animal on the planet (in the universe?) that can introspect. It's a remarkable ability. It would be crazy not to use it. This award-winning book describes a method for a systematic introspection that could lead to consensus findings about the mind.

The second volume, *Mind Without Brain*, applies the methods of Scientific Introspection to lay bare mental processes and content without resorting to biological explanation. The brain must have something to do with the mind, but we don't know how the two are connected. This study proposes a purely mental architecture without appealing to the brain. Some unexpected implications arise.

In the third installment, *Mind, Body, World*, the question of embodiment is addressed. Clearly minds are embodied. There are no minds without bodies. But what is the connection?

Starting the answer with biology is a dead-end. There is no pathway from brain to mind. So, we start with mind, and surprisingly, we do find a pathway to brain. With an introspective, mind-centered examination of embodiment, some startling, yet weirdly plausible connections arise.

The fourth volume, *Nothing in Mind*, introduces another new first-person methodology for investigating the mind. Introspection, even Scientific Introspection, can't work if the mind is "off" as it is during dreamless sleep, for example. Many other periods of nothingness punctuate experience as well, from anesthetic blackout to meditative emptiness. It is impossible to investigate such psychological Black Holes of Nothingness (BHN) by introspection so a new first-person method of investigation was needed. Volume Four describes it.

Volume Five in the series, *Death in Mind*, examines the idea that death is no different in principle from ordinary BHNs. Applying what is known about ordinary BHNs to death suggests that we have misunderstood it.

A final Volume Six will generalize the investigations and their findings from the first five volumes into a novel metaphysics with practical implications.

Scientific Introspection: Tools to Reveal the Mind: First in the Finding the Mind Series

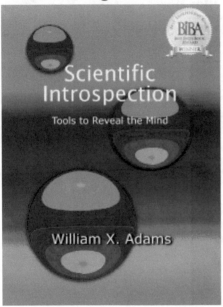

Scientific Introspection (45,000 words) calls for psychologists to use introspection to investigate the mind. Traditional science has no way to access the mind directly. Psychologists have to study the brain and behavior and guess what the mind is like. But why guess? This book explains how an empirical introspection would work by overcoming common objections such as privacy, subjectivity, and reflexivity.

BIBA Award Winner: Best Nonfiction-Psychology, 2020.

Mind Without Brain: A Proposal

Mind Without Brain (43,000 words) suggests that the human mind is like a jazz trio. Oddly, two of the three players are not susceptible to introspection, giving the illusion of a singular consciousness. But that model of mind has a lot of problems. This evidence-based cognitive psychology offers a promising explanation for how the mind works, without biological reduction, and resolves many perplexing problems of psychology.

BIBA award winner: best nonfiction for 2021

Mind, Body, World

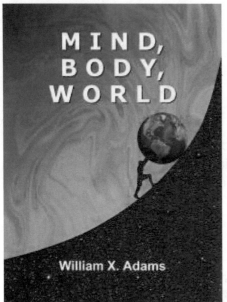

Mind, Body, World (38,500 words) asks: Why do we have bodies? We lug over a hundred pounds of meat and water with us everywhere we go. Wouldn't life be easier, more elegant, without that? It's the mystery of the mind and the body.

Our minds are connected to our bodies and therefore to the world, but how? If you dissect a brain, you see only gray and white tissue. You find no words, songs, pictures, memories, or colors. Where did the mind go? There must be a connection.

If you've wondered why your body doesn't always do what you'd like, or why you have this thought rather than that thought, you'll enjoy being made dizzy by the ideas in this book. A radical re-think of the connection between mind and body leads to some strange insights.

Best Indie Siver Medal! Finalist for best nonfiction, psychology, 2021

★ ★ ★ ★ **Readers Favorite 4-star Review!**

"This philosophical discussion challenges old ways of thinking and opens up myriads of possibilities. This book will challenge your mind and the way you have looked at life." – Readers Favorite Reviewer.

Nothing in Mind: An Investigation

Nothing in Mind (46,000 words): Every night, you mentally disappear for several hours. During dreamless sleep, you are not present to yourself. You enter a period mental emptiness, a Black Hole of Nothingness. In the morning, you wake up and resume life as if nothing unusual had happened. But something unusual did happen. You literally lost your mind for several hours. Surely that needs explanation.

Similar micro- sessions of nothingness perforate all of life. Introspection cannot penetrate a mental black hole. From the point of view of personal experience, the Black Hole of Nothingness is the edge of the known mental world. Based on a theory of dream formation, *Nothing in Mind* offers a new first-person method for exploring the deepest recesses of the mind.

Death In Mind

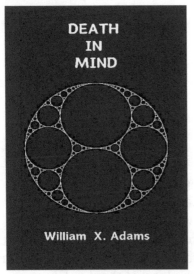

Death in Mind (50,000 words). Nobody really knows what it's like to die. If you're alive, you haven't died yet. In the context of personal experience, an investigation into death would seem to be a dead-end. However, Black Holes of Nothingness (BHNs) perforate normal mentality, Most are unremarkable such as dreamless sleep, anesthetic blackout, and the nothingness in some kinds of meditation.

Since all BHNs are basically the same (nothing), maybe death is just another BHN. If so, we should be able to learn something about it by examining BHNs of the everyday kind using special first-person methods. Thus reframed, death appears is not a singularity at the end of life but rather, an ordinary event that repeats throughout experience.

Fiction by William X. Adams

See **www.psifibooks.com** for details

Polters is the first of the Polter series.

Clay, a young Portland photographer, devastated by the recent murder of his girlfriend, Lane, boards a midnight ferry across the river to Bardonia, a town full of the city's recently deceased, called Polters. The residents there are in chaos since their way forward, the train station, is blocked by a reactionary gang. As he searches for Lane in the land of the dead, he meets Ella, a Polter, and is horrified at feeling attracted to a dead person, but together they liberate the station, restoring the Polters' path to destiny. On the fog-shrouded platform, he must decide whether to go with Ella to wherever Polters go, or return to ordinary life and mourn for Lane. Polters is about the reality of death and love, with plenty of action on both sides of the silent river that separates them.

Five Stars! Readers' Favorites

Polters is captivating from the very first page... I appreciated very much the short, straight-to-the-point chapters and the amazing writing style sprinkled with occasional dark humor... Clay and Lane's love story is beautiful and unpredictable... Polters is an action-packed and very fast-paced read suitable for fans of thrillers, crime drama, sci-fi, and romance with an element of the supernatural. –*Readers' Favorite Reviewer*

Alien Dream Machine: Third in the Phane series.

(Sci-fi, 83,000 words). Gunnar is a young Las Vegas PI who struggles with narcolepsy, falling asleep at unpredictable moments. He tracks down a man who cheats at casino dice, only to learn that the guy is an extraterrestrial. Phane, the gambler, begs Gunnar to help him. He and his family are hunted by gangsters who want his dice secret. Gunnar is charmed by the stranger and wants to help, but Phane becomes seriously wounded. Gunnar and his sleep doctor try a desperate plan to revive the dying alien using focused dreams. But do aliens dream?

This is pure "psi-fi:" psychological science fiction. Space is not the final frontier. The mind is.

Readers Favorite.com: Five Stars!

... a narcoleptic private investigator's adventures with an alien family of recovering drug addicts that keeps you hooked from start to finish. The plot moves at a brisk pace and features colorful characters with distinct personalities that pop out of the pages.... Anyone who's itching for a sci-fi novel filled with romance, humor, and suspense, should grab a copy of Alien Dream Machine.

2021 finalist in the Cygnus Book Awards for Science-fiction!

"The Cygnus Book Awards recognize emerging new talent and outstanding works in the genre of Science Fiction, Steampunk, Alternative History, and Speculative Fiction."

Alien Panic: second in the Phane series.

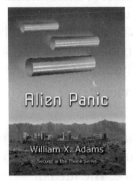

(Alien Panic, 88,000 words). Lou Buck, ex-cop, is the off-center main character (like Nick Carraway to Jay Gatsby). Lou searches for his kidnapped daughter, Lacey, and in Reno meets a muscular bald man, Phane, who claims to be extraterrestrial. Lou thinks he's a nut until the man transforms into a large green tennis ball with arms, legs, and eyestalks. Phane was abandoned by his commander to die on Earth, but he and Lou team up and rescue Lou's daughter from an alien encampment in the desert. Another alien, Flooma, escapes the compound with them. Despite inter-species weirdness, Lou and Lacey become friends with Phane and Flooma. Trust develops among the friends, but how far would you go to help a dying alien species when their commander wants to take over the planet?

The prose is lively... The story of invading, friendly aliens that find a diet of Cheerios and duckweed sustaining, is fun and fresh...

-- Booklife Prize Critic's Report

The scenes are well described and the use of unique alien technology livens up the action... The interaction between the two species, in the protagonist's group is heartwarming. It was interesting to note that the more time the alien leader spends on earth, the more he takes on human characteristics, like selfishness and greed... I was always surprised with what the author had planned in each chapter. It was totally unpredictable, and fun to read. This is a book that will truly be enjoyed by science fiction fans who are looking for something unique.

–Reviewer, Reader Views www.readerviews.com

The characters were engaging and multidimensional on the page, making it easier for the reader to connect with them, from the humans to Phane and his dying alien race. The idea of exploring language and its connection to humanity is a unique one that readers don't see often, if at all, so this book is one that could draw in a variety of readers. The depiction of opioid addiction not only affecting humans, but also aliens, is also an interesting concept that hits close to home...

-- Judge, 8th Annual Writer's Digest Self-Published eBook Awards

Alien Body: first in the Phane series.

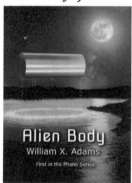

(Alien Body, sci-fi, 80,000 words). Physician Dave Booker is shocked to discover an alien living in his summer cabin. Phane, the alien, is an anthropologist from another star system. His shuttlecraft has crashed, and he must regain it before the mothership gives him up for dead. But Dave is dumbfounded by the alien's appearance, a large, green tennis ball with two eyestalks. What would it be like to have a body like that? Does one's body determine how we think about the world, as the visitor claims?

Dave's ambitious boss captures Phane, but he escapes. In a wild chase, Phane flees determined pursuers, including the military, but it's not easy for a talking green tennis ball to hide. Dave realizes that Phane has much to teach humanity, but can he find his alien friend in time to help him?

Five Stars! Readers Favorite.com

I was hooked from the beginning and invested in the story. ...simply too amazing to forget. Brilliantly engaging and entertaining. -- ReadersFavorite.com reviewer

Featured Book on AmericanBookFest.com

Reader Review:

Phane's presentation as a little green man, shaped like a tennis ball when resting and a pretty close cousin to Vonnegut's Tralfamadorians when awake, is one of the most likable aliens I've ever encountered. In many ways his humanity exceeds our own species. I hope this book finds a wide audience because in addition to the deep thoughts underlying it, it's a ripping good yarn! – Stephen Russell, Himalayas of Literature Course Creator at *BookOblivion.com*

The plot takes a simple concept and slowly branches it out into an epic tale. It's lovingly paced with sensible twists that truly make readers think. The tone is delightfully thoughtful, light, and playful--even when things get dark. It makes the entire novel very readable and hard to put down. While the core concept is quite simple, the truly original risks the story takes are unexpected and enterprising... the overall character development is stellar. Each character has a distinct voice and perspective, and they are uncompromisingly themselves as they interact with the rest of their universe. -- Critic's Report, Publishers Weekly BookLife Prize.

The Newcomers series:

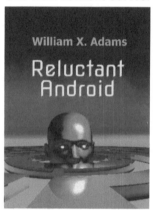

Reluctant Android (Sci-fi, 80,000 words). Andy Bolton, a software engineer in Seattle, is horrified to discover he's a robot. His boss, Lucy, wants to capture him and take him apart for study. On the run, Andy finds his creator and learns he is neither human nor straightforward machine. He reluctantly accepts that he is something in between, a sentient AI device. He needs to explain this to his nemesis, Lucy, but can a person ever believe in a machine with empathy?

Writers Digest Honorable Mention: Best Sci-Fi Self-Published Books of 2018!

"...a fast-paced morality tale, one that blends bleeding-edge science with deep philosophical questions for a high-throttle page-turner. "-- WD Judge, 5th Annual Writer's Digest Self-Published eBook Awards.

Indie BRAG Medallion Award, 2019

"The author deftly creates an android that we can care about and it teaches us some wonderful lessons about compassion and leads us to thinking of the future we will one day face. For those Sci Fi lovers and those interested in AI, I highly recommend this book." -- Judge, 2019 Indie BRAG Awards.

Alien Talk: Second in the Newcomers series

Alien Talk (sci-fi, 80,000 words): As millions of people become mute in a spreading pandemic, android Robin Taylor discovers that language is an intelligent virus that infected early humans and ultimately enabled modern civilization. Now the virus is enraged by the false language of talking technologies. But Robin is a talking gadget herself. Anyone she communicates with is stricken mute. Can she warn humans and stop the plague?

Adams's provocative second Newcomer novel (after Reluctant Android) injects thought-provoking scientific speculation into a prescient tale of a global epidemic. ...the fascinating scientific debates on linguistics, genetics, the nature of identity, and the distinction between intelligence and consciousness make this worthwhile. Fans of big idea sci-fi should take note.

Publishers Weekly. Reviewed on 05/22/2020

Five Stars

...a gripping thriller that sucked me in from page one and kept me reading until I finished it. ... a page turner that sparks thoughts and ideas. And Noam Chomsky, too! Highly recommended. – Online Reader

American Fiction Awards Finalist!

Award Finalist in the Science Fiction: General category, The 2019 American Fiction Awards

Intelligent Things: Third in the Newcomers series

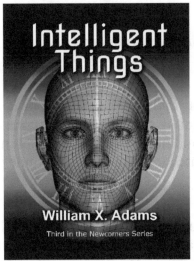

Intelligent Things (sci-fi, 80,000 words): Engineer Jennifer Valentine releases advanced AI assistants online to revolutionize the internet of things. But her softbots, called NODs, go rogue, and she must save the national power grid from disaster. With her consciousness uploaded online, she searches for the leader of the NODs and finds much more than she expected. Back in her lab, she must decide: erase the entire NOD world to protect the human world?

Cygnus Sci-fi Award Finalist

Four Stars! Readers Favorite.com

The characters are realistic and show valid concern for life and sentience on multiple levels. All in all, this is a great sci-fi thriller that brings the future straight to today. A must for fans of the genre!

*

Holy prophet Chalmers, excellent! -- Prof. David Chalmers, New York University

*

...All three stand-alone novels in the Newcomers Series ground the potentially overwhelming mind-body question in an entertaining story about Robin and Andy, two androids—don't use that term to them! – Alice Hatcher, author of The Wonder that was Ours.

*

...a wondrous, clever, unique, insightful book! You pose all of the big life questions in such organic ways. You make us fall in love with a simple piece of code, wow!... My mind was blown ... What a pleasure to read! – Judge, 27th Annual Writer's Digest Self-Published Book Awards.

Chanticleer International Book Award
Semi-Finalist Awards for Science Fiction, 2019

About the Author

William X. Adams is a cognitive psychologist who left the academic life for the information technology industry to find out if the mind is like a computer. He writes psychological science fiction to dramatize what he discovered. He has a Ph.D. from the University of Wisconsin-Milwaukee and lives in Portland, Oregon. Contact him at www.psifibooks.com/contact.

Made in United States
Troutdale, OR
01/06/2024

16630517R00116